FIRST GENERATION WHITE COLLAR

A practical guide on how to get ahead
and not just get by with your money

L. MARIE JOSEPH

Printed in the United States of America

Cataloging-in-Publication data for this book is available from the Library of Congress

First Edition 2010

Published by Moshire Press
P. O. Box 941672
Atlanta, GA 31141
www.moshirepress.com

Joseph, Linda
  First Generation White Collar: A practical guide on how to get ahead and not just get by with your money/ Linda Joseph

ISBN: 061539082X
ISBN-13: 978-0615390826

2010915250

To my husband Arry, who never cease to amaze me and to my daughter Chelsea, I look forward to teaching you my financial principals

To my parents, thanks for choosing to love me

Acknowledgements

I would love to thank everyone that helped put this book into fruition. Before, I did not know how to get started in writing a book and each one of you help me along the way. It takes more than one person to work on a book. I could have never launched this book without my team guidance. I want to thank Dan Baum for giving me the title of this book. Looking back, the title I originally had was not a good fit. We came a long way since the first draft. Thanks for giving me direction and a target audience. Thanks also to my team of editors at Create Space, great job! I'm grateful to J. Steve Miller for advising me how to take my time when it came to making decisions about publishing. I want to thank the lady on Bancroft Street that introduced me to fine living. This book started with you in mind. My siblings for teaching me life lessons, I learned from your mistakes and successes. As the youngest of seven children I sure did learn a lot. My parents for listening to my dreams of being rich, I'm glad you listened to my goals even though I was a little arrogant. I would like to thank several financial bloggers. I probably would have not written a book if it wasn't for you guys. I'm indebted to my loyal readers of my blog; the purpose of writing a book is to give my readers good information on personal finance and money management. Special thanks to Seth Godin for returning every single one of my emails, yes I know I asked a lot of questions. Mary Brown, my website designer—big thanks- the site I originally had sucked! For more information and resources visit www. firstgenerationwhitecollar.com

Preface

Wealth is the ability to fully experience life.
-Henry David Thoreau

On Halloween night in 1982, one of my older sisters took us trick-or-treating on the "other side." I was nine-years-old, and I'd never crossed the boulevard to the upper middle-class subdivision of Park Island. Our own neighborhood of little wood bungalows contained all I knew about the world. But my sister had gotten the notion that the treats from the upper class might be good, so without a word to the grown-ups, we scampered across the boulevard. We skipped the first house because the lights weren't on. At the second house, the older kids ventured up a broad, brightly lit porch while I hung back, worried. The door opened on a short little old lady with a froth of bluish-white hair. But it wasn't the lady who caught my attention; it was the space behind her. I had never in my life seen a house so big. The foyer was the size of my bedroom, the chandelier, its crystal lights shining gloriously, as big as an easy chair. A wide staircase with gleaming mahogany banisters curved up like a set from Gone with the Wind waiting for Scarlett O'Hara to swoop down. I'd never seen a two-story house, much less a mansion. As we trooped to the next house, I asked, "What does that lady do for a living?" My sister shrugged, interested more in the fine chocolate she'd received and the prospects for more. If I'd had the nerve, I'd have run back and knocked again, to ask the old lady. Instead, I walked backward, gazing at the pool of light playing softly on the columns, the porch, and the neat rows of shrubs.

That was the day I decided to be wealthy. My parents worked hard—my dad as a longshoreman on the New Orleans riverfront and my mom as a homemaker. They made a good life for their seven children because Dad was good with money. He carried no debt, and he saved. He'd paid off the house by the time he was in his fifties. He even contributed to help us go to college.

Like a lot of people of my generation, my siblings and I were the first in my family to go to college and the first to achieve the white-collar life. But as I look around, I notice that while we first-generation white-collar workers are making more money than our parents ever dreamed of, many of us are somehow not living as comfortably as they did because, as a generation, we have burdened ourselves with crushing debt. We have student loans to pay off. We have mortgages—many of them bigger than we can afford. We're making car payments. We're paying off the furniture, the appliances, and the vacation. Our credit-card bills grow frighteningly every month. Instead of building wealth for future generations, we're going ever deeper into a hole. For all our achievement of getting up and out, and going to college, many of us risk falling backward.

It isn't entirely our fault. We first-generation white-collar folks may know all that the best colleges have to teach us about sales, business management, computer science, or medicine, but we don't know squat about money. Most of us weren't raised by people sophisticated about managing it, and didn't absorb lessons of thrift and investing with our mothers' milk the way people born to the white-collar life did. And when we graduated, we faced financial lives way more complicated than our parents'. While Dad's employers did the financial work for him—managing his life insurance and pension plan—we have to negotiate the wild world of IRAs and mutual funds on our own. While Dad had the only type of mortgage available to anyone—a thirty-year-fixed rate—we have to choose among five types of mortgages and cope with pushy real estate brokers more than glad to "educate" us about them. While Dad was influenced in his consumption by his longshoremen neighbors, we're bombarded with cable, Web, and social-networking come-ons to buy everything from Audis to mcmansions. Surrounded by friends and family who respect and honor us for being the first to go to college, we are eager to prove to them that a college degree bestows wealth. In many ways we are set up to fail because we are flush with incomes unimaginable to our parents, yet unprepared and unequipped to manage it. At risk is nothing less than our family's toehold on the American dream. We may come out of college dreaming of the white collar, but we soon strap on the iron collar of debt.

Despite Dad's sober, hard-working and debt-free example, I slid out of college and straight into that iron collar. I got a good job as a technical services specialist, earning $27,000 a year. Though I already had to come up with $100 every month to pay off my student loan, I borrowed $15,000 to buy myself a shiny new car. Feeling flush with my slick salary, I also loved to dine out, buy clothes, and take vacations. Before I knew it, I was living paycheck to paycheck—and falling behind; my checking account balance stayed under $100.

Luckily, I remembered that Halloween-night promise I made to myself and set about getting a second education—a financial education in which I was the teacher as well as the student. I went to the library and bookstores, and read every book I could find on the subject of money: financial independence, debt-to-income ratio, budgeting, retirement, investing, fast money, slow money, getting rich, becoming a millionaire. I listened to audio books and podcasts. Some were okay, others good, and a handful excellent; I got so I could tell pretty fast. Instead of shopping, I spent every weekend cramming, taking notes on how to make, spend, and save money. I was a personal-finance addict.

At thirty-one-years-old, I bought my first home; yes, it was a lot like the old lady's on the other side—a four-bedroom with two stories, a big foyer, and a dazzling chandelier. Yeah, baby! I also had savings and an investment account, and a year later, when our daughter arrived, I opened a college fund for her. By the time she was two, I was not only saving and investing but also treating myself to plenty of vacation travel and dinners out.

This book is about how you, first-generation white-collar like me, can build the habits you need to have it all. Don't get me wrong: this is no get-rich-quick scheme. It's a start-simple-and-build-steady scheme. I will urge you to think of your first five or ten years out of college as a stint in the army—short on luxuries but essential to achieving your long-term goals. If you're smart enough to finish college and enter the workforce, you can be smart enough to amass wealth. Whether you are black, brown, or white, as first-generation white collar, you share with me both a unique responsibility to your family and a terrifying vulnerability to the iron collar of debt. But you also share the aptitude to adapt. You have the talent to earn. You can learn the skills to live in comfort, ease, and stress-free luxury.

First Generation White Collar addresses the growing number of vulnerable young professionals with earning power but no financial savvy. Statistics, often concentrating on minorities, show what targets we've become:

Families of color have been found to add on debt at a rate that substantially exceeds their increase in income, thus decreasing the wealth-building potential of every dollar earned.

A National Community Reinvestment Coalition study of mortgage information from 100 metropolitan areas in the United States recently showed that, for example, in Hartford, Connecticut, minorities were much more likely to own a high-cost mortgage than white home owners. The difference was greater for middle-income blacks than for low-income blacks.

African American families are using financial resources that could be used to achieve financial security to meet increasing monthly interest payments, hampering savings and acquisition of assets like real estate. Above-average debt lowers credit scores and drives up interest rates, so it's a vicious spiral.

African Americans mostly accumulate debt by purchasing things that depreciate in value like cars, furniture, electronics, and appliances. Traditional redlining by banks means that high-interest credit cards are among the few easy sources of loans for minorities.

But it's not just minorities. It's a question of culture, and first-generation white professionals are often equally vulnerable.

A recent Fisk University study showed that half of all Fisk students coming from households with incomes below $55,000 faced the obligation to send money home, consequently taking on more debt than they could handle.

While their peers with professional parents tend to learn financial skills before they left home, we have not had time to develop an ethos and culture of savings and investment. They are in a hurry for wealth, and often mistake its trappings for its true comforts: security, stability, and yes, stress-free luxury. They need to learn the lessons of patience and financial nurturing that they didn't acquire growing up—and they need to learn it fast.

Problems often start in college—whether it's taking out too many of the wrong kind of loans or avoiding loans entirely and missing out on opportunities. These problems multiply when graduates use a new-car purchase to show the proud family they've arrived. If you've experienced some of these problems, I understand. I've been there. In this book, I'll give you practical tips to help you get out of financial bondage and move toward your dreams.

Table of Contents

First Generation White Collar

L. Marie Joseph

Chapter 1: Debt

Paying off Debt

You just graduated from college and accepted your first white collar position, or perhaps you're already working in your career and notice that it's easy to make money but harder to keep it. Now what? You should now concentrate on paying on your debts, saving for short-term goals and investing for your retirement. Upon graduating from college and entering a white collar job you're now living a comfortable life. Yeah right. Now is the time to tackle your money scars. According to Bankrate.com, college students average $2,200 in their credit card balances. Graduate students have more than double that amount. Most young professionals begin their careers with debt.

Credit cards
(The wealth snatcher)

TransUnion credit reporting agency, says that 33 percent of Americans pay their credit cards off in full every month. So I guess the rest of us cannot handle our debt load. About 70 percent of us have no business owning a credit card. What if the rules were to change and it says you cannot charge any more items until the previous bill is paid in full? About 70 percent of us would not have a credit card. More of us would have money to save or invest if we didn't have so much outstanding debt. Debt cuts into our earning power. Once we earn money, it goes to creditors instead in our pockets and bank accounts. If you carry a balance on your card, cut up the card. Do not charge anymore until you have demonstrated you can pay off your debt obligations. Once you incur a balance, the banks start to make money, and you begin to lose money.

I personally do not have a credit card. You know it's funny that when you are in the habit of paying with cash/a debit card, you really don't miss credit. I love to travel, and I think a credit card will give me permission to travel without having the cash. It can make you easily slip into debt. I choose not to slip. Maybe in the future I will own a card, until then I will keep my life simple.

Being a first time white collar professional, we tend to prove to our family and peers that we have graduated from college, so, yes, we buy things—mainly big tickets items.

Having this new money all of a sudden can overwhelm a first generation white collar. We are faced with all these options that were not there before. And America is not helping by marketing to us every single day to spend money.

Your plan should be to pay yourself first before spending it on wants. What happens is that we tend to live a certain lifestyle so long that we cannot wait to get a job with a high-five-figure annual salary and reward ourselves by spending and going into credit card debt.

> *When I first graduated from college, I had a great starting salary. So the first thing I did was put my new wardrobe on a credit card saying to myself I will pay it off once I get my first paycheck. I never stuck to that plan. Now I'm a professional with over $40,000 in credit card debt.*
>
> *Lori K., 34*

Personal Loans
(The cousin to credit cards)

Personal loans can also snatch your wealth if you let them. Like any other debt, they take money away from you. It's best to avoid getting a loan altogether, but if you must borrow, remember that the longer the term, the longer you stay in debt. The shorter the loan term, the better gain you may have.

Retirement loans:
(The kid next door that you barely see)

Since this is informal debt, we tend to think it rarely exists. About one in every five Americans had an outstanding loan in 2005[1]. Again, the shorter the term, the better. I know that almost every personal finance book will tell you not to borrow from your retirement because if you become laid off or switch jobs you have to pay it back in full within sixty days. I did not follow this rule. I went against conventional wisdom.

I once borrowed from my retirement account back when I was in my twenties. I borrowed $1,000 because I needed to get new tires for my car, and I could not wait any longer. Each day I was praying that the tires would not go flat. They had very little tread. I did not have enough in my savings account to replaced four brand new tires. So I borrowed it from my 401k. The tires did not cost $1,000 but that was the minimum amount that I could borrow, I had the money within a week. I purchased my tires. I paid the money back within the two months. I had them take out $350 per pay period. Did I suffer for those two months? Yes, do I regret it? No. However, I learned from this lesson to keep a nice cash cushion of at least $1,000 for emergencies.

---

1   *Employee Benefit Research Institute*

The point is if you're going to borrow, try to make the term as short as possible. Would I do it again? No, I learned from that incident to have money in the bank to provide a cash buffer, so I will not have to raid the 401k. But if it is a true emergency that cannot wait, you may have to use this source. It makes no sense to be faced with a foreclosure, and you have the money sitting in a retirement account. Just make sure you have a plan to pay it back quickly.

You can take out a loan for virtually anything such as cars, houses, pets, and vacations. It can be all yours in form of a loan. The biggest issue with loans is that if you're not careful or educated with credit, you can mortgage your future. You don't want to spend months paying back something that you are not using anymore.

I believe all debt is just debt. There is no such thing as good debt and bad debt; one just is less expensive than the other. However, credit cards are the most expensive debt. They are short-term loans. If not paid within thirty days, it can cost you interest, late fees, and finance charges. When credit cards were first introduced, they were intended for emergencies only. Now it is used for everything but emergencies. Credit card companies had to find a ways to keep you using your cards constantly, so now there are reward points, cash-back bonuses, and vacations to promote usage. People now use their credit cards for everything from a pack of gum to European vacations. They even found a way for you to shun debit cards by making you feel more protected against fraud. Debit card has the same protection as credit cards. VISA debit cards have the same protection as VISA credit cards. MasterCard also has protection on its products.

Whether you using a credit card for education or a business, just remember it is not your money. Don't overextend yourself. There are always options: you could attend a less expensive school or start an online business instead of having a brick-and-mortar store. A loan is money that is owed and has to be repaid at some point. Also consider the consequences if you don't finish school or your business fail. Do you have a plan B? Borrowing money maximizes the risk. It's one thing to have a failed business and it's another thing to owe creditors <u>and</u> have a failed business. When you have outstanding loans it becomes harder to move ahead.

Loans can make you overextend yourself. We tend to spend more when we don't see the money leaving our hands. Most people live for today and suffer the consequences for their actions later. Being educated financially can make you breathe easily and not be saddled with debt. Think twice when taking out a loan. Ask yourself, do I really need this or is this a temporary want? Can I get this later by saving the money? Can I get a less expensive alternative that has the same effect?

I think the older we become, the less we should depend on debt. As our income grows less debt becomes necessary.

Debt is an evil plot to keep you poor -Seth Godin

Student Loans

I paid for tuition all on my own, all sixty thousand dollars. That set my net worth back by sixty thousand dollars by the time I started working my first real job out of school

-S.I. 26, blogger

You must be careful when borrowing money for school. Because the money is so plentiful, we tend to borrow more than needed. Be prudent when taking out loans for school. Make sure your total debt equals to the first year of pay out of school. Once you start your white-collar adventure, you want your first year salary out of school to be equal or more than your total student-loan debt. My professor, Dr. Clara Wiley reminded us of this when I was in college. For example, if you have $40,000 in student loans upon graduation, you want your first professional job to pay $40,000 a year or more; if it doesn't, you may want to change your major or borrow less.

Here is a story of two people that looked at student loans differently:

Henry and Maria

Henry, twenty-three-years-old, borrowed more than enough money to attend private school in Louisiana. He came out of college with $50,000 debt. Henry's first job out of college had a salary of $38,000 plus benefits. He went out and got a super cool apartment in a swanky part of town and super cool furniture on credit. He was a sharp dresser—thanks to MasterCard. He later met a young lady and impressed her with dining at the best restaurants and nightclubs. As a desperate measure he began taking cash advances from his credit cards to pay bills. His income was eaten up with payments to creditors: car loan, credit cards, and Sallie Mae. What a life. He was barely thirty-years-old and now over $70,000 in debt. Not able to afford a home, Henry became depressed. Henry went overboard. Borrowing $50,000 to make $38,000 a year makes no sense. Always research the beginning salary of the major field of study you are going into.

Maria, nineteen-years-old and a freshman at a small college in Texas, was afraid to borrow money at all for college and dropped out. Once she figured out that her grant was not enough to cover the entire tuition for the year, Maria wanted to go to college and earn a degree to become a psychologist she dropped out because she became discourage by the five-figure debt it was going to take to finish college. She later realized jobs that don't require a college degree paid just enough to get by. Frustrated that she is only getting by and not getting ahead, she regrets not taking out loans and grants to go on to college. By not taking a risk by investing in her future, she paid a bigger price. Sometimes playing it safe is not the wisest move.

In Henry case, he went overboard when it came to student loans. Had he done a little research on the starting income of his major he either would have picked a less expensive school or changed his major. Find a happy medium when it comes to education. Not applying to college at all can also be a risk you cannot afford.

Rule of Thumb: Borrowing money for education makes sense if you do not borrow more than you can expect to earn in a year at your first post-college job.

If you are having difficulty making your student loan payments, you can try consolidating all your loans to a lower interest rate. This will make the payments lower. If you want to eliminate your student loans altogether, there are programs that can help you ease the burden:

AmeriCorps, Peace Corps, and VISTA are all volunteer programs that can erase your student loan debt. These volunteer programs usually require you to have a two-year commitment. If you choose to volunteer make sure you are willing to commit. The best time to do this is right after you graduation from college, while you are young and have less responsibility. Also there are government programs such as teaching in an urban community or practicing medicine in a low-income area.

Another option you have is **deferment**, which means the principal and interest payments are deferred, the maximum limit of a deferment is three years. The last option is **forbearance.** Unlike a deferment, forbearance allows you to make payments only on the interest, and the principal is temporarily postponed.

Check with your student loan servicer to see which option is best for you.

Housing and Other Consumer Debt

Let's take the average first generation white-collar couple:

Pedro and Ayesha lived in a one-bedroom apartment on Madison Street in a leafy suburb of Atlanta. Pedro, a dark-eyed soccer player who is one of the funniest men I've ever known, had graduated with a computer science degree from the Georgia Institute of Technology and been snapped up by a software firm downtown. He'd gotten a raise within six months, with praise from his boss as someone who not only excelled in his code writing but also raised morale just by being himself. Ayesha, who'd graduated with honors from Spelman College, loved her work in a small interior design firm. She was also a dynamite cook. Her friends craved her party invitations, and we'd cram into their kitchen to watch her attempt a soufflé or crowd onto their little balcony for a gourmet barbecue. Pedro and Ayesha were one of the happiest couples. Between them, they earned $85,000 a year, which was way more than their parents ever earned in their lifetime.

Ayesha likes to say it was her artist's eye that got them into trouble. She quickly grew tired of rearranging the furniture in their third-floor walk up. She wanted a new canvas to paint on. She wanted space, a patio, and a garden. "Windsor Castle would have been perfect," Pedro jokes. "Or maybe the Biltmore."

Their mortgage broker, at a friendly company in a little brownstone right in the neighborhood, was encouraging. He crunched the numbers in the usual way, figuring they could afford two-and-a-half times their yearly income. Within a week, they were approved for $212,000! Approved!

They were ecstatic. Pedro called his family in Florida, and congratulations came pouring in. Ayesha's mother asked about their student loans, their car debt, and their credit cards. "She's a worry wart," Ayesha chuckled. Her mother doesn't have a credit card, and she's never owned a new car. So Ayesha dismissed her mother's concern.

For the next month, Pedro and Ayesha spent weekends driving the nearby suburbs of Atlanta, Georgia until they found the perfect subdivision in a Decatur neighborhood it was a brand new subdivision. The playground was well maintained, most of the houses were already occupied, and the last three acres were just being built out.

They chose a model that came in at $210,000; it was on a corner lot and had just enough space for Ayesha to have the flower garden she'd dreamed of. The agent for the subdivision, a slender, well-dressed man who wore a nice polo shirt with khaki slacks of a golf professional, sat them down in the office and pulled out the forms.

"Now, how about upgrades?" he said, and smiled.

Pretty soon Ayesha was choosing granite countertops, crown moldings, and stainless steel appliances. The cost now stood at nearly $230,000.

Back they drove to the mortgage broker, who told them they couldn't get a thirty-year, fixed-rate mortgage for that amount, but he could put them into a 2/28 adjustable-rate mortgage. By the time they moved in, Pedro and Ayesha's monthly note, between their loans, mortgage, property taxes, and home owners insurance, was $3,000. That was three times more than what they'd been paying in their rental apartment, and it left barely enough for them to buy groceries. Ayesha made one more mistake, falling in love with the Lexus that the guy across the street pulled up in every evening. "Hey," said Pedro, "I'm not going to say no. We were living the dream." Ayesha upgraded from a Toyota Corolla to the Lexus 450 she felt was appropriate to the neighborhood, boosting her car note by $350 from her previous car note.

Within twelve months, Pedro and Ayesha were falling behind in loan payments they'd always made on time—the specter of foreclosure was looming. "Pedro stopped making jokes," Ayesha said. "I'd never seen him so worried. His mother could hear it on the phone, but he couldn't talk to her about it. Even his boss commented on it. The life was just going out of him."

Here are a few mistakes Pedro and Ayesha made:

1) Planning—or the lack thereof. Pedro and Ayesha could have calculated the expenses that came with owning a $230,000 house and decided that they would look for a house in, say, five years. That

way, they would have had a goal to look forward to. Without that goal, Ayesha felt trapped and claustrophobic, and let her emotions lead them into home-ownership.

2) Falling for upgrades. Pedro and Ayesha could have anticipated the sales pitch at the subdivision's real estate office. If they'd known they wanted upgrades, they might have started with one less bedroom or a smaller lot. But they decided on the house first and reached for upgrades as an afterthought.

3) The adjustable rate mortgage (ARM). This was a classic beginner's mistake. There are five basic kinds of mortgages, and three of these should be avoided at all costs:

Adjustable Rate Interest Only Mortgage

Pedro and Ayesha got a 2/28 ARM, which meant for the first two years they would only pay the interest on a thirty-year loan and for the other twenty-eight years they would start paying on the principal and interest. The adjustable rate comes into effect after the two years have expired. So yes, Pedro and Ayesha would start to pay down the principal, but depending on their line of credit, their interest rate would go up. You might end up behind where you'd be if you were paying rent. Compare that to a low-interest fixed-rate mortgage, in which you are paying down the principal and your interest rate will never go up.

Negative Amortization Adjustable Rate Mortgage

Just when you thought an ARM was ridiculous, here comes this mortgage product. The payment option ARM allows home owners to choose each month how they want payment to apply to their home loan. Each payment option is crazy for this type of loan:

1. Interest Only - Again, payments are low at the beginning but creep up on you like a thief in the night. Interest only means

you're only making payments on the *interest* not the principal. Your balance is not being paid down. You are making no progress.

2. Principal and Interest - It might sound sensible, but remember, in this kind of mortgage, interest rates can shoot up.

3. Minimum Payment - Don't ever get sucked in by this one. Every time you make the minimum payment, the difference between the minimum payment and the interest-only payment is piled onto the balance of the loan. Huh? That's right. It's crazy. The loan balance will never go down, only up.

Balloon Mortgage

These are mortgages in which the full cost of the loan is not spread evenly over its term. They promise low interest payments in the short-term but ask for a whopping—balloon—payment down the road. A balloon loan that matures in, say, five or seven years requires payment on the entire balance in that time. Again: crazy.

Two Good Mortgages

The other two mortgages— – thirty-year fixed-rate and fifteen-year fixed rate—are okay, as long as the amount falls comfortably within your spending power. It didn't for Pedro and Ayesha: even if they'd had a "good" mortgage, the amount was bad because it took them to the edge of a cliff. Don't leave it to a mortgage broker to calculate for you, as they did. The broker will be comfortable selling you more than you can afford because it's not her money!

My friend, Pam, a mortgage broker, described the kind of first-generation professionals who are bound to get into troublesome mortgages. "It boggles me that so many young adults feel the need to have mcmansions as soon as they get married, knowing that it took their parents years to afford a home. They want everything up front—the degree, the marriage, cars, and a house. It's all about instant gratification, and it makes them suffer in the long run."

I tell you this story because these are the typical mistakes that first-generation white-collar professional's make. When you stretch yourself financially, one little emergency can put you in a hole. Of course, no one thinks of that when things are going good.

Ayesha could have taken out a smaller loan by asking herself these questions: do I really need this or is this a temporary want? Can I get this later by saving the money? Can I get a less expensive alternative that has the same effect?

Sometimes our eyes are bigger than our pockets, and once we are on a roll there's no stopping us.

When my husband and I decided to buy a home, the loan officer kept saying that as time goes on both of you will get promotions and raises so the mortgage payment will only be a squeeze temporary. I'm like "yeah right"

When my husband and I buy a big purchase that requires a "debt" contract, I always think of the negatives (the what ifs) not the positives.

I think of layoffs, divorce, pregnancies, downsized incomes, emergencies, and wanting to quit my job to follow my calling.

I think of all the things that can possibly happen (and they will happen) over a thirty-year period. Most may happen over a ten-year period.

Well, you may wonder who thinks of all that when buying a house? I do. It's not common to think of a divorce when you're buying a house, but I have to wonder if he can still afford the home or can I still afford the home if one income disappears.

So when you enter a purchase that requires a contract to pay over years and years, always ask yourself: could I still afford it if something major happened? Do I have a backup plan, i.e., savings and good job skills?

Never go by what a salesperson says; you are responsible for yourself. It's not their job to look out for YOUR best interest. They're just trying to make money.

Small World   by Tom Briscoe

3-23 © 2004 BRISCOE   www.briscoe.org

If you already have debt, why do you need to tack on more? Have patience and wait.

Having a house note and a car note is enough; when you tack on the credit cards, personal loans, and other debts on top of your normal day-to-day expenses, it all can drown you financially. Now you are chained to your job—what a life to live.

All because you have to let the world know that you make a nice income. That's not cool

What's cool is $10,000 in your bank account, your children are secure for college, and a family that loves and respect you. Wealth is not about money only; it contains human and intellectual elements as well that money can't buy.

If you just inherited $10,000 and have no idea where to put it or how to use it wisely, you will indeed lose it. This is why income really doesn't matter; if it did, every millionaire would have stayed a millionaire. You need the right assets, and family, good friends, and financial skills to manage your money correctly are the assets that complete you.

Most of the time, it's not a money issue it's more about our habits. We have to change our relationship with money. Your habits are what brought you to where you are financially today. If someone wiped out your debt and gave you a second chance, most of us would go back into our old habits. Everyday people pay off their credit cards with a home equity loan and what happens? Later they run up the debt on their credit cards again. So now they have a home equity loan and a pile of credit card debt.

So it's not the debt, it's usually us! If you can get your debt under control (meaning your debt-to-income ratio is under 20 percent), you can breathe more.

Example:

Credit card one $200/month

Credit card two $120/month

<u>Car $400/month   </u>

Your monthly debt payments are $720

Your monthly income is $4000

720/4000 = .18

Your debt/income ratio: 18 percent

Which is a decent number, obviously you want to get it to zero, but for now this is manageable.

Credit should be used sparingly for things such as furniture, cars, and boats. Please pay cash for depreciable goods if you can. If you cannot pay cash for the item, your next option should be to take out the shortest term loan possible. By doing that, you must put down the largest down payment possible.

Also credit should not be used for short-term consumption such as gas, food, impulse items, or vacations. These items should be paid for with cash or if financing, within the first 30 days after the purchase to avoid interest.

Why would you want to add 18 percent interest on top of your vacation expenses? It doesn't make sense. Don't make your financial life more difficult than it should be.

The less debt you have, the more income you can keep for yourself. Have discipline when it comes to credit

Save to Fend off Debt

Having money saved can avoid future debt payments.

Some people are able to save for retirement before they can save in a bank. Why? Because our employers take the money directly out of our paychecks preventing us from having physical access to it. What a splendid idea.

So why don't we do this with our saving? Have your bank automatically take it out of your checking account the day after you get paid. Manually taking money out of your account and transferring it may not work.

The IRS and your retirement account are funded by taking money from your paycheck; why not feed your savings account in the same way? Everyone needs a saving account for emergencies. Calling parents or depending on friends gets old after awhile. After all, you're a white-collar professional now. Depend on yourself from now on. Save yourself from yourself. Start an account.

> *No matter how well laid out a plan is, there are going to be setbacks. For example, it's common for emergency funds to be needed before they are fully funded. Many people hit that first setback and assume all their planning and effort wasn't worth it. If a single setback causes you to give up on your financial plan, you never committed to it in the first place*
>
> *-Jeffrey Strain*

What percentage of my income should I save? Glad you asked. I recommend 30 percent. Holy crap—that's a lot! Yes it is, but this book is about you being wealthy not average. As I said before, if you want to be average, do what everyone else is doing—don't save and accumulate debt.

Yes, it's easier to spend 30 percent than to save it. Everyday we fight spending money versus contentment in America. We are hit with enticing product marketing, and our peers, neighbors, and friends don't help much.

When I was fresh out of college, I simply wanted to get paid just enough to save, invest, pay bills, and still have enough money leftover to spend the way I want afterward. For a while I had enough to pay bills and spend but not enough to save and invest. Now ten years later, I have enough to do it all. Hey, it only took a few years, but it remained my goal.

My strategy is to avoid credit card debt—not credit cards necessarily, just the debt. Credit cards give you permission sometimes to overspend this causing you to get into debt. Also stay away from the mall because it will cause you to recklessly spend. Stay away from toxics that cause you to spend more than you need to. Practice that for at least two years.

Now most people (especially women) are not going to do that for two years. But that's what I did, and the results were more money in my bank account.

Keep practicing smart spending, and you'll be surprised how much you can put way. During this stint, I had few friends. Who wants to hang out with a girl that has five outfits in her closet? I was not flashy during this hiatus. I got my hair professionally done once every three months and wore Payless shoes until I could not wear them anymore. I wore clothes from outlet stores and also from discount retailers. Yeah, I know that doesn't sound sexy, but my bank was all the sexiness I needed. I seldom wore makeup, but hey, I did take a shower everyday, and my clothes were presentable.

I also did not have fancy perfume and wore the same dress to different events. Oh no, not the same dress. Most women hate that. As time went by, my bank account was growing.

Eventually I did upgrade myself and bought the best makeup, clothes, and, yeah, perfume. I did not feel guilty because I was able to do it without touching my savings, since I had no debt; I did this with the cash flow from my income

Priorities first, then fun

I am now giving more to charities and giving nice tips when I dine out. I do not abuse the malls because I have years of smart-saving habits to keep me out of debt. I think it's harder to break a person from spending than making a saver spend. Once you understand the gimmicks and marketing of certain companies you will be less apt to spend and more apt to invest.

Not sure what debt to pay off first?

List your debts in order of payments (or maybe in order of annoyance)

Creditor	monthly payment	balance
Credit card	$400	$10000
Car loan	$340	$4000
Personal loan	$333	$5400
Home equity line	$200	$25,000
Student loans	$80	$20,000

It shows that your credit card debt is the biggest payment. So if you think in terms of freeing up your cash flow, you may want to start with that creditor. However, if you want to knock out the balances quickly by paying extra on the smallest balance, you may choose to pay off the personal loan since it has the lowest balance.

The reason why I did not list interest rates is because it does not matter when you are paying extra on debts. Focus on knocking out the debts! Not interest rates.

Add up all you debt balances and monthly payments. Figure out what works best for you. The end goal is to pay off all consumer debt completely; it may take two or three years for some people. Just remember the purpose of this is to free up cash flow. Think of how much cash you will have to save and invest each month once debt is paid off!

The choice is yours. Some people want to free up cash flow, so they can have more money in their pockets; others may want to knock out the smallest balance first to feel like the getting traction faster.

If you want to skip conventional wisdom and pay your debts in order of annoyance so you can sleep better at night, you may do that as well. For example, if you owe the **IRS**, (Internal Revenue Service), you may want to start with them first. The reason for this is that their interest and penalties add up much quicker than paying late on any other bill.

Also if you owe a **traffic ticket**, you may want to pay it off first before any other debt because if you don't pay you may be looking at a warrant for your arrest!

Other annoying debts maybe a pesky uncle that you owe money to or a meddling mother-in-law!

Lessons Learned

-Avoid credit card debt if possible
-Stay away from wants (temporarily)
-Keep your debt-income ratio as low as possible in order to build savings
-Practice contentment

You need to practice all four in order to save

Chapter 2: Saving

Saving money is so essential. It's always good to have a cash cushion. It always makes life smoother. There are people who save just enough to stay afloat and there are people who save more because they want to get ahead financially.

Save 30 percent of your income (if you want to be wealthy) and force yourself to live off the remaining 70 percent. That includes taxes, medical insurance, expenses, and other needs.

You cannot do that, you say? Start with saving 10 percent. I always say push yourself to the limit just to test your discipline level. Most people cannot save 30 percent because they have debt. Oh there's the D word again, I told you it cuts into your savings. If you were to save 30 percent, where should you direct it? Good question.

10 percent emergency savings
10 percent retirement
10 percent giving or future purchases

As a first generation white collar professional, we are faced with all these options that were not there before. And America is not helping by marketing us every single day to spend money.

Your plan should be to pay yourself first before spending on wants. What happens is that we tend to live a certain lifestyle so long that we cannot wait to get a high five-figure a year job and reward ourselves by spending and going into to credit card debt.

You can switch it up, however, you want.

5 percent giving

5 percent purchases—large purchases such as a car or kitchen remodeling

10 percent emergency savings

10 percent retirement

Whatever your priorities the point is to get into the habit of saving a percentage of your income regularly.

> According to David Bach's *The Automatic Millionaire*, if you save:
>
> 5 to 10 percent of your income you will be middle class
>
> 10 to 20 percent of your income you will be upper middle class
>
> At least 20 percent of your income you will be rich
>
> See where you want to be financially and strive to save it!

Ric Edelman, financial adviser and radio show host of the Ric Edelman Show has another way to look at saving.

[i]If you are putting 10 percent of your pay into your retirement and have a 3 percent match, that is counted as 13 percent of your pay going into a 401k plan. Social security counts as well, and it makes up 7.5 percent of your pay. So altogether you have 18 percent going to retirement. Your 10 percent can really be 18 percent once you add in the match and social security deductions. So you maybe further along than you think.

[i]*podcast on 8/22/09, The Ric Edelman show*

Budgets Schmudgets

I never lived on a budget simply because they do not work; it's easier for me to pay myself a percentage of my income and start spending from there. I save 30 percent of my income and work with the remaining 70 percent. After taxes and medical insurance, it's more like 50 percent for most people.

I personally save 30 percent of my income, and it goes to charity, retirement, saving, and my child's education account. It's much easier for me to automatically skim off the top rather than making a list every month to allocate how much food I can eat and how much to put in my gas tank. Paying yourself first is the best method.

Now, of course, this method is easy when you have no debt payments. Try to get your debt-to-income ratio under 20 percent (see chapter 1). Once that is done you can afford to do the 70/30 method. Work on your ratio first. While working on your debt ratio continue to save a little.

How Much Do I Need in My Emergency Fund?

Depending on your personal risk, if you are the only breadwinner in your household, it maybe six months of household expenses (not income).

Expenses are the amount of money needed for your household to operate. However, if you are single with no dependants it can be two to three months.

You decide your comfort level. If you have an extremely secure job such as a federal employee or a school teacher, you may only need two to three months of expenses saved. Less secure jobs should have more than three months.

> *"It's better to have money and not need it than to not have it and need it."*
>
> *-Les Brown*

Emergency Savings Can Be Used for:

Car trouble, medical expenses, or unexpected job loss

You cannot save for three months of expenses overnight. I would start with one month of expenses. Make that your first goal in saving.

"I would save _____ a month from my income. By March, I would have one month of savings." By December, I will have four months of emergency savings." I will obtain this goal by decreasing _____ and increasing _____.

Make sure your goals are attainable and specific to your personal situation.

This is your responsibility! We are responsibility for our own financial life. Thirty percent of your income is the goal that you should shoot for. These are the three common saving buckets that you need:

Retirement
Upcoming expenses
Emergency savings

Retirement is considered *long-term savings*, emergencies are *short-term savings,* and then there are *life expenses.*

You can direct more to one savings buckle and less to another.

Retirement includes:

401k, 403b, IRAs

Upcoming expenses to save for may include:

College savings
New car

A new pool
Education
New appliances
A wedding
A divorce?

Emergency Saving

Savings accounts are for emergencies and having cash available for the unexpected. That's it. What you save/invest in addition to that becomes your wealth

Most people spend more when times are good and spend less when times are bad. What you need to do is save money when times are good, so it will be there when times are not so good. This is what wealthy people do. When this business is doing well, they save; other businesses give out big bonuses, and you wonder why they become bankrupt a year later. You have to balance everything. We don't think about saving until we hit a bump in the road. Not being able to save when you in fact have the money is a sign of laziness, and we all know nothing comes to a lazy man. Don't wait for a layoff or recession to start getting smart with your money, save when things are going good.

Save your money and one day it will save you

-African proverb

Prepare before you need to. I know having money sitting in the bank that's not being used is pretty boring. It does not suppose to do anything. It's there to be available when an emergency occurs. Boring? Yes, but worth it. I know it's hard because everyday is a temptation to buy something. For example, you have $5,000 in the bank for emergencies and Home Depot comes out with this state-of-the-art refrigerator that has everything. It's shiny and attractive, no one else you know have a refrigerator like this because it just came out. And it's only $2,000. You have five grand in the bank. You know you have the money, you are gainfully employed, and everything is going well. So technically, you don't really have anything stopping you. You say to yourself. "I can get it out of savings and restock the account later with my income. So you pay for the refrigerator. So now you have $3,000 in the bank. A few days later, your transmission goes out, and $3,000 is gone or you become unemployed through no fault of your own. These things happen, so don't try your luck. If you really want that $2,000 fridge, save for it. Who knows by the time you have saved the money, the price goes down or better yet, you may not want it anymore!

Once you have saved, invested, and paid your bills, you can spend. Just take care of important things first, before you start spending money on your wants. I really don't suggest that you have to save three to six months' worth of expenses first before you have a little fun.

Personal finance is not all strict; it can be fun as well.

I don't want you to think by reading this book you may think you cannot have any guilty pleasures. Where is the fun in saving money when you're not able to enjoy little of life's luxuries? Everything needs to have a balance, just don't overindulge.

Emergency and retirement funds are absolutely should be mandatory to have. Home remodeling and brand new gadgets are not needs, but it indeed enhances your quality of life.

If you're a home owner you should save for remodeling projects. You should not take out a home equity line against your home. If you don't own a home and want to one someday, the quickest way to get started is to pay off past due accounts and stay current on any payments you may have. Always have a cash cushion for emergencies. Once that is complete, you can start saving for a home of your own. Once your consumer debt is eliminated, you need to set up automated accounts. Designate a certain dollar amount or percentage of your income to allocate toward these goals.

Retirement and college accounts are considered investment accounts and should be kept at brokerage firms. Investing is meant to be long-term goals that are over five years. Emergency savings and upcoming expenses are held in savings accounts because they are usually short-term goals under five years.

Most 401k retirements accounts can be directly taken out of your paycheck if you work for a company. A Roth IRA can be setup online or by phone with a brokerage company and can be set up as an auto draft from your checking account. They are flexible and you can set the day each month when funds will be taken out your account.

College savings can be in the form of a 529 or an ESA educational plan and are available at a brokerage firms such as Vanguard or T. Rowe Price.

Here is a sample of how your financial life should operate:

Your Financial Empire

This is a pay-yourself-first model. You can change the numbers and goals to reflect what is important to you. Just have a plan to organize your money where you want it to go. The choice is yours;

you can spend it, invest it, or save it. Make the right choice with money. Don't go *ballistic* on payday. Set up a financial empire, and **you** tell your dollars where to go.

Where to Put This Emergency Account

Having a savings account at a credit union or bank is common. However, if you are not disciplined and are addicted to immediate gratification, you may want it as far away as possible. A money market account may be better for you.

I personally like ING DIRECT. *ING DIRECT* does business online, over the phone or by mail. If you make a withdrawal it takes two business days to process. That's how long it takes to have access to the funds—it's not immediate. At a credit union or local bank it takes two seconds to process your funds from the teller to your hands.

With Internet banks, such as ING you can simply make a transaction online or by telephone.

There are no major pros or cons; it all depends on how near you want your money. In selecting a bank, make sure it is federally insured by the Federal Depositors Insurance Corporation (FDIC). Credit unions should be insured by the National Credit Union Administration (NCUA).

How to Allocate the Funds

You can set up subaccounts that are housed under your savings account through www.ingdirect.com or by calling them 1-800-*ING-DIRECT*.

This is an example of automating subaccounts. Here is a snapshot of a savings account. Once you login into your savings account, this will appear:

ABC Savings Account

Subaccounts	Balance
New kitchen remodel	$500.00
Car repair fund	$250.00
Vacation fund	$1100.00
Christmas fund	$50.00

So if you were to allocate $400 to your savings account and want it disbursed to subaccounts it may look like this

You have monies in each subaccount making your total balance $400. You can do this on a weekly, bi weekly, monthly, or the fifteenth and end of the month basis. Subaccounts can help you become more organized with your money.

You can also automate your credit cards bills, student loans, and your mortgage payments to each creditor. Simply call your creditors and have them automatically draft your bills on the day you are paid or the day after. Or you can do it yourself through bill pay with your bank's checking account.

Chapter 3: Investing

This subject can be foreign to us as well. Investing can be very intimidating if you have never done it before.

Why pay a broker to seek out investments?

If you do not know about investing, stick to an index fund. Index funds are a mixture of stocks (small, medium, and large companies).

They track about 500 American companies, so if you buy an index fund, you're buying a piece of 500 American companies. Instead of two or three hot stocks that someone told you would make you rich. Index funds have so many companies that it lessens your risk.

If your employer does not offer index funds as a part of your 401k, it's because it does not take a manager to manage these funds. So there is no management fee. Index funds have very low fees because you do not have to pay a manager to manage the fund. Mutual funds charge fees because someone actively manages them. A 401k is more interested in funds that charge high fees because it has to make its money some type of way.

Mutual Funds: Flee the Fee

The thing with mutual funds is that they have several fees, including plan administrator, sales charge, management, redemption, and 12b-1 fees. My advice is to try to find a mutual fund with the lowest fees possible: something that has a zero before it would be nice. An expense ratio less than 0.99 is preferred.

"Remember 85 percent of funds perform less than average the S&P 500 average."

The perk with a 401k is the employer match, so take advantage of it. It also tends to help you pay for the fees. The only time a 401k is bad is when there is no match, and the mutual fund choices are filled with high-expense ratios. When that is the case, you may be better off going with a traditional IRA or a Roth IRA where you can choose and control the funds. I prefer you to max it to the employer's match and use any excess cash to invest in an IRA.

Where to Invest

If you do not know where to direct your money when it comes to investing, here are some of my favorite investment companies:

T. Rowe Price   www.troweprice.com 800-225-5132
Fidelity   www.fidelity.com 800-544-9797
Vanguard   www.vanguard.com 800-992-8327

Why? Because they all have long track records, which means they have managers who have been managing the same fund for at least five years, low turnover rates, good performance, and, oh yeah, low fees. If you cannot find that type of satisfaction with mutual funds, try electronic transfer funds also known as (ETFs).

If you can muster up $600 a month and invest it in a mutual fund that averages 8 percent a year, you will have $44,380.04 in five years.

Too much? Try $300 a month—still too much?

I don't believe you, you may have it, and it goes to that big thing in your driveway that has four wheels or that home project you financed with a home equity line of credit (known as a HELOC) that could not wait. Or maybe it's those plastic things in your wallet that is taking up your $300. You have it; it's just diverted to other bills.

Imagine if you had $9,000 in the bank and no debt. Can you invest $300.00 a month—that's $150.00 a pay period? Yes. The debt makes it harder to save, but when you have a reason to save, you will be more likely to cut corners and make it happen.

Income + Savings = Wealth

From now on this is your new formula. Keep repeating this in your head. If you get discouraged write $44,000 (or any amount with which you're comfortable) down and look at it everyday. Again this book is about wealth, not finding ways to just get by.

Income + idiotic spending = debt

Avoiding consumer debt can help you accomplish your goals more quickly. Idiotic spending will slow the process. By having $44,000 saved, you can buy a car with cash or a go on a Caribbean vacation with a new wardrobe or maybe provide a free ticket for your children's education.

Whatever your goal, SAVE for it. Don't wait for your lottery number to be called or for an inheritance. Start now. Replace the word *financing* with *SAVE*. I guarantee you will begin to have fatter pockets. Idiotic spending will guarantee empty pockets.

Discipline = good results

At the ripe age of thirty-one, I had a four-bedroom home, very little debt, and an investment account and savings.

At thirty-two, I added a college fund for my daughter. At thirty-four, I was doing everything I wanted, saving, traveling, and dining out almost every night. I'm able to accomplish this by sticking to my formula: Income + Saving=Wealth. You do not have to be retired to enjoy life; the earlier you start, the quicker you can enjoy your life.

Remember you only want to start investing if you plan to not touch your money for at least five years or more, *i.e., college funds, retirement.*

When investing in a 401k or IRA you should spread your diversification mainly over four mutual funds there are: international, large cap, mid cap, and small cap funds. You can also opt to hedge against inflation, meaning you can add Real Estate Investment Trusts (REITS) and precious metals (gold, silver)--no more than 5 percent. When you pick your mutual funds in your 401k plan, you do not want to put all your contributions in one fund.

Standard Portfolio

15 percent international
25 percent small cap
25 percent mid cap
35 percent large cap

This is a simple standard portfolio.

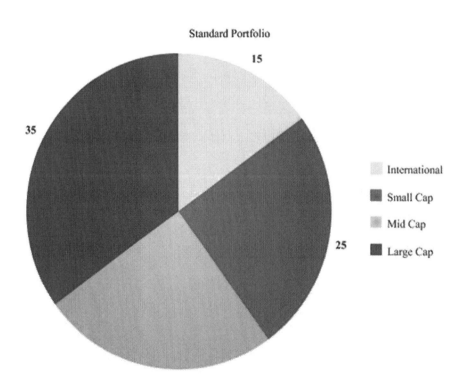

W/REITS and/ or precious metals (for inflation)

5 percent REITS
5 percent precious metals (gold, silver)
10 percent international
20 percent small cap
20 percent mid cap
40 percent large cap

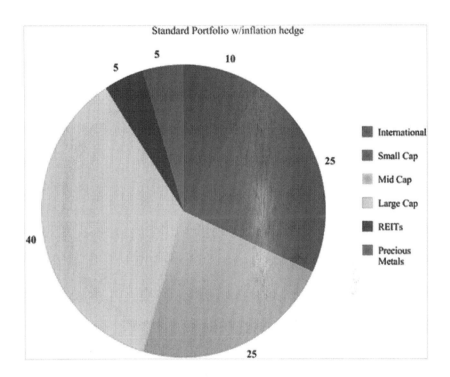

As you near retirement, you may want to gradually rebalance a percentage of your portfolio to something less risky like cash or bonds

35 percent bonds or cash
25 percent mid cap
35 percent large cap
5 percent international

The risk is not as aggressive. It is more conservative.

The past three sections I have discussed the past, present, and future about your money.

Past: Your Debts

Everyone has a past—the day you bought that sexy new car, when you financed your education, when you bought clothes on credit. Although these things happened in the past, you may be still paying for it, which makes it hard for you to live in the present.

Present: Cash (in the bank)

What do you have to work with now? Having cash in the bank can be a buffer against the emergencies and *the inconveniences* of day-to-day life. It makes life and the ride in life more smooth and enjoyable. Having cash gives you a sense of security and insurance policy for current mishaps.

The Future: Retirement Accounts

Your 401k investments are future needs. Most people do not work forever. Therefore, you need money to be there when you can no longer or prefer to no longer work. Whatever date you have set, make sure this fund has the right amount of money, so you can relax and be comfortable

In order to save, you must avoid carrying debt, especially credit card debt. In order to invest, you must have money saved first. So you have to be consistent in this order: pay off consumer debt, save to avoid having to create new debt, and invest to get rich.

You should be currently paying on your consumer debts—more than the minimum. This will get you in a position to build up a cash cushion. Once you have a cash cushion that you are comfortable with, it's time to get ahead in life! Start investing. Manage your debt, save for important things, and invest smartly: you can do this one at a time or all three simultaneously. Each person is different. Some like to attack chapters one at a time or all at once.

In order to get ahead you must avoid consumer debt, save, and invest a percentage of your income!

Now that we know what, how, and where to save and invest our money, all that is left is to figure out how to control and manage our spending and lifestyle.

Spending It and Keeping It

You are a first-generation white collar; start off on the right foot with money. So you can pass on the knowledge of personal finance to your children.

Pay off your debt and increase your income so you can invest more.

The best way to get ahead with your money is to figure out how much it cost to operate your household needs. If there is additional income, you can use the additional surplus to save and invest your income. Always earn more than you spend. That is the key. Imagine if you have no consumer debt to add to your household needs. You'll be amazed how debt can impact your life in a negative way. When you live simply, you are less stressed. Figure out what is needed to operate your household. You will find out it can be very little.

Let's take for example a couple the only has their mortgage and living expenses. Let's call them Mark and Mindy:

They are newlyweds; both are in their thirties, and both are college graduates with white-collar professions. Combined they have a household income of $75,000. They also have $23,000 in student loans, $15,000 in car debt, and $400 in credit card debt. Their total debt is $38,400. They're only contributing 3 percent of their income to retirement savings because most of their income is going to rent, utilities, and debt.

After being married for a year, they decide to set their first goal: to pay off their consumer debt in two years. They put $1,600 toward their debt each month. Through focus and persistence, they manage to pay off their debt in nineteen months because they put their income tax refund and Mark's bonus check toward their debt. After they paid off their debts, they decided to bump up their savings and retirement funds. They are now contributing 10 percent of their income each to retirement and also 10 percent of their income to savings.

Now let's take another couple, Jack and Jill:

They both make the same salary and have similar debts as Mark and Mindy. However, they have a different ending. Although they already have debt, Jack decides that he wants to upgrade his car, and Jill agrees; they go out and buy a bigger car that comes with a bigger car note: $300 a month more. Jill figures that if he has a car, she can go out and buy that Fendi handbag for $400 that she saw at Neiman Marcus. She gets to the store and realizes if she purchases the handbag on a Niemen Marcus credit card she can instantly get 15 percent off. So she applied for the card. She was approved for $3,000. Now at this point her handbag seems small compared to the credit she has available. So she picks up more items such as designer lotion, perfume, jeans, and some suits for work. All in all she accumulates $2,000 of "stuff."

Fast forward, two years, they are still making the minimum payment on their debts. Since the majority goes to interest, they have only paid off 35 percent of their total debt.

The difference between these two couples is that one had a plan and the other did not. Simply by working together and having goals can make or break a young marriage when it comes to money.

It gets worse; Jack is laid off and because they did not have a plan to pay off their debt, it is increasing because Jill cannot afford to pay all the bills on her own. The interest rate rises on all credit cards and late fees start to accumulate.

So if you're just starting out in life or soon to be married instead of having a big wedding and a gorgeous house, you may want to start slow, with a nice wedding and maybe rent for awhile.

We always tend to rush out and buy everything. So we can be on the same level as our parents instead of starting slow. DON'T RUSH INTO DEBT! It's not good for a young marriage. Your goal should be to pay your debts.

It's not going to kill you to live with only a few basic necessities for a few years. Most people exaggerate the word *comfort*. They live a life with luxuries and think it's just comfortable. Change the way you look at comfort.

Comfort	*Luxury*
A sofa	a designer sofa
A car	a Lexus
A refrigerator	a stainless steel digital refrigerator

Change your mentality. You have plenty of time to buy what you really want once you get rid of your debt.

When you make enough income that surpass your needs you will have positive cash flow, instead of being in the hole every month. The problem is that once we increase our income, we increase our wants. So now we go right back to where we started, and we have more stuff but are still living paycheck to paycheck.

The median value of a college graduate's primary residence was $280,000

-Survey of Consumer Finances, 2007

Most college graduates earn enough to meet their needs financially, but because of debt, they never have disposable income. My suggestion is to sell stuff that you no longer need, pickup temporary work, or freelance. Challenge yourself to make enough on the side to pay for your liabilities. When all else fails, you may just need a better paying job.

Live simply until you can save enough buy things outright with cash. Want to get there faster? Create more income through raises, bonuses, a promotion, a side business, or part time job. That can shave a few years off being in debt.

Remember, debt can mess up this goal of simple living. So avoid debt, if possible.

Set goals. Stick to them. Avoid toxics, such as the joneses, debt, and anything else that will sidetrack you. Read personal finance books, and engage yourself around debt-free people (this maybe kinda hard in America) or people with that are doing better than you financially. Don't know anyone. Search the Internet for personal finance blogs. Start with one of mine, www.moneymonk. net. The power of association can gear you to having the right mindset.

Now, of course, there is daycare, health insurance, and occasional dining out. Not every household is the same when it comes to basic needs. Creating an extra income stream can close the gap.

Here is a short list of side businesses that can help you boost up your income without quitting your day job.

These businesses require little or no startup capital:

Consulting: this is simply helping a company or individual with things that can enhance their business. Freelance writing, computer work, advice on accounting, etc.

Dog Walker: Busy people do not have time to do this, if you're a dog lover, set your hourly rate and go for it.

Lawn Care: planting flowers or cutting grass, this can be big business especially during the spring and summer. Pass out flyers or give discounts to people that have been referred by a client.

Day Care Services: Love children? This can be a nice cash cushion for you. You just need a few toys, a nice fenced backyard, games, healthy snacks, a hot meal every day, a first-aid kit and a license to get started.

Bookkeeping: Many small companies need a bookkeeper; you can work from home in most cases. An average bookkeeper can make $50 an hour.

Seasonal Tax Preparer: You can seek employment at HR Block or Jackson Hewitt or you can start your own company.

These are just a few, find your talent and prepare to prosper. Freelance writing, tutoring, or a caretaker also requires little or no capital.

It took me several years to get to the "comfort level." If I were to ask you if you'd like to have $6,000 in cash by next year? The only caveat is that you have to put away about $500 a month into an investment account, what would you say? If it's too much to sacrifice, change the numbers. Find whatever number you are comfortable with saving. The point is to change your thinking! Redirect a percentage of your paycheck or earnings to investments after you free up your debts payments.

In order to invest more have fewer debts.

Don't over leverage yourself. If you have a home mortgage and a car note, guess what? You're overleveraged! If you and your spouse both have car notes, you're overleveraged. Try to have one debt at a time if possible. You always can afford the car note the day you buy the car; we never look into the tune up and other maintenance that a car brings. Add insurance and gas on top of a monthly car note, and you will have a heavy load. Keep it simple.

Chapter 4: Get Smart About Spending

Forty percent of parents have bailed their adult kids out of debt at some point. Auto loans 40 percent / Credit Cards 30 percent

- CBS Money Watch

Usually if you cannot save or invest it's because your expenses exceed your income. When you are stuck in that boat, there are only two things you can do: *increase your income or cut expenses.* I can tell you that in most cases it's not our income—it's the debt we have that creates more payments. Car note, credit cards, and personal loans all cut into our disposable income.

Having a cash cushion in the bank and no consumer debt should be your ultimate goal. I know it may take you two years or more in some cases, but what else you have to do? Being financially free of revolving debt is something to strive for!

Most people get paid, pay their bills, and live off whatever is left. Reverse that method and pay yourself first by adopting the seventy/thirty rule (see chapter 2). You know exactly what you have to live off. With technology, you can make all this automatic. Have your savings and retirement automatically deducted from your bank or paycheck. That way you don't have a chance to spend it.

Let's discuss the biggest expense that keeps us from obtaining a healthy savings or investment account.

Housing

So now you're making a great salary and have a college degree under your belt. Now your eyes are getting bigger. You want a house! That apartment you have is starting to become a prison cell. Please don't become like Pedro and Ayesha.

A home is usually the biggest expense we have. That being said, try your best to qualify for a mortgage that has a fixed rate, you don't want any surprises down the road. You want to also have a payment that is under 30 percent of your income. You know this is going to be your biggest expense, so try to make it as low as possible. Your loan should also be limited to a fifteen- to thirty-year debt sentence.

For example if your take-home pay is $5,000 a month, your monthly house payment should be no more than $1,500 a month. So let's not get house fever and buy something $2,000 a month because it looks better. Get what you can afford! You want to be able to pay for house payment AND save and invest comfortably. Not just pay your house payment and expenses. You always want to build wealth while you are paying your home off. Stick to renting if your payments will be more than 30 percent of your income. You do not want to own anything that will jack more than 30 percent of your income.

Ideally, you're the price of your home should be two and one-half times your salary (two times if you want to be wealthy). Don't fall for what the mortgage company tells you can afford. They do not know your personal situation. Divorce, sickness, and layoffs can all happens during the life of the loan. Always think of these factors when agreeing to a contract for so long. No one is immune to Murphy's Law. Mortgage Brokers will not discuss these issues with you. It is your responsibility to education yourself.

"Education is when you read the fine print. Experience is what you get if you don't."

-Pete Seeger

So if you make $50,000 a year, and the mortgage company approves you for $200,000 —RUN. This is four times your income, and you cannot afford it.

Depending on where you live, this can vary; I have friends in Washington, DC, and New York, and they cannot comfortably make this happen. If you live in a large, high-expense state, such as California or New York, your percentages may be slightly different.

Interest only and adjustable rate mortgages (ARMs) should always be avoided. ARMs almost always adjust higher not lower. You should always get a fixed-rate mortgage. You don't want any surprises down the line.

Rule of thumb:

-Take out a fifteen- to thirty-year mortgage
-Make sure the payment is under 30 percent of your income, if you want to be wealthy.
-Having a mortgage payment that's below 30 percent of your household income gives you more room to save and invest.
-Seek financing through a credit union or your local community bank.
-Interest only and ARMS mortgages should be avoided.

Negotiate on Large Purchases

Next to a house, a car is the second largest purchase you will make. When buying a car don't just go out to the closest car dealer and purchase a car. You should shop around for at least thirty days. Start off by visiting your local credit union. They usually have the best rates. They are less likely to rip you off than a local dealer. Local car dealers go through several banks to get you approved. What's wrong with that, you might say? If you have to hear a lot of no's to get a yes, that is not good for your interest rate or buying power. If a bank rejects you, it is because you cannot afford the car based of your income and credit. Going to more banks means they are willing to rip you off on the interest rate because they are dealing with below average credit. Car dealers also tend to stretch out your payments beyond four years. Some car dealers go as far as a seven-year car note.

When you buy a car, don't go for the four-year term. Try to knock it out in two and one-half years or maybe three at the most. The quicker you get rid of the car payment, the quicker you can free up cash flow.

When buying a car, please keep it to less than four years. No one should be enslaved to car debt longer than that. Tell the finance company upfront that you want a three-year payment plan. They can do this for you. If you cannot handle three-year payments, that car is not for you. A car payment over three years can interfere with your wealth building.

> *Most of my customers are middle class that only wants to know one thing. They are the ones that ask "How much a month?" rather than "How much is the car?"*
>
> *-Max, car salesman in Louisiana*

Of course, your first option is to pay cash for a car. If you want to build wealth having no car note is one way to have extra cash to invest or save. However, if you must finance keep the terms as short as possible. Less than four years is ideal. You can visit a credit union or community bank for financing. Try to avoid getting financing through a car finance company because they often give you longer terms. Research online (via bankrate.com) it will tell you the average interest rates for a (new and used) car loan. These rates change constantly.

Once you are approved for a low interest rate, you can start shopping for a car in your price range. Try to keep the price under the amount for which you are approved. There are always taxes, insurance, and other fees associated with buying a car, make sure you budget for all of this. A car should cost no more than 10 percent of your income. That's right 10 percent of your household income. This makes the payment and insurance easy to pay.

Here are the rates for auto loans:

Auto	Rate
48 month New Car	6.26%
48 month Used Car	6.39%
36 Month Used Car	6.52%

Average annual percentage rate as of July 2010

Visit at least five different car dealers. Remember just because a car is x amount of dollars does not mean that is the price you are willing to pay. Dealers can always go down on the price. Avoid hidden fees such as extended warranty, paint sealant, credit life insurance, and GAP insurance. You do not need these extras; they can add hundreds to thousands of dollars to your final price.

Negotiate the price and terms up front.

Recap:

Paying cash for a car is your best option

If financing, your car expenses should be no more than 10 percent of your income

When financing, go to a local credit union or community bank

Avoid finance companies

Financing on any car should be less than four years

Don't forget to budget for car extras such as taxes, insurance, and gas

Resist retail temptations:

Try to have more discipline when it comes to spending money; remember you are IN CONTROL. The purpose of a shopping center is for retailers to market their products and for you to spend your hard-earned money. All retailers mark up their products, so they can make a profit. For instance, if it costs them $20 to make a shirt, you better believe they would charge you $60 or more for it. Yes, we all need clothes, but we do not have to keep up with the trends constantly. If we do, we will stay broke and in debt. Beyond high school, I doubt if anyone cares what name brand of clothes you wear.

Try to stay neutral by wearing solid colors. Stay away from loud colors that only look best during spring and summer months. You want something that you can wear all year round; a yellow floral shirt may not be a good pick. Also, keep a pair of multipurpose shoes, particularly black or dark brown that can basically go with everything. I know this may not be easy for women, but remember this book is about getting ahead and not about impressing others.

Homemade facials may replace several trips to the beauty shop. A little baking soda, warm water, and a drop of baby oil can work wonders. Rub into a paste and spread gently on your face, leave on for ten minutes, and rinse off. This once a month routine can work the same as an expensive facial. Also Crisco can make a good moisturizer, no kidding.

Go to the park or library if you want to be entertained not the mall. Worry more about what you put in your brains rather than material stuff. It will change your thinking and make you more intelligent. Read books than can enhance your relationship with money. Learn how not to spend frivolously; stop reading fashion and lifestyle magazines, it will only make you want more, and you will never be satisfied. I know that old habits are hard to break, but something has to change for you to have a better relationship with your money.

America wants your money, and they will find every tactic to get it. Your first priority should be to beef up your savings and retirement account and avoid retail consumption.

Retailers are making it so convenient for you to buy; if you don't have the money, they will politely direct you to a credit card application, and you can get it now. Just think about it, if you do not get that shirt, hat, wallet, purse, or shoes right now, what is the worst that can happen? You will continue to use the ones you have. Don't worry you're not going to die. These things are not emergencies. So stop trying to act if they were. You want to beef up *your* bank account not the retailers'. Buy what is reasonable not the latest gadget, and you will see you account balance grow. Do this by paying yourself first, then bills and then the retailers (wants). People that are in debt are usually in fear, and fearful people are not in control of their money. Don't fall in this category. Buying something on sale does not mean you saved money. If you choose to not buy it at all, then you have saved money!

Remember these frugal tactics are not for you to do for the rest of your life, there is always a time to splurge. I just want to show you ways to not have instant gratification. Make your savings account a top priority.

Lifestyle Inflation

Awww…it creeps up on us little by little. This is the number-one mistake that most college graduates make. The day they receive their first paycheck, they usually have an excuse to consume the entire paycheck. They spend money on all the things they dreamed about while they were in college.

> *The day I entered the professional workforce, I went out and financed a BMW. I never though about how the monthly payments would affect my life. There were plenty of times I had to skip nights out with friends because more than half my income was going to transportation costs: gas, upkeep, insurance, and the car payment*
>
> *-James C, 29*

I remember when I was in my twenties; my rent was $400 a month. I had a one- bedroom apartment. Everything in there was given to me or bought used. Once I got married and had children, it all changed. I wanted a better car and a of course a house. A one-bedroom apartment and catching the bus was no longer exciting to me as an older person. As I moved up in jobs and income, so did my lifestyle. So of course we had to buy a house. After I had a baby, I went out and got a $400-a-month car note. So why did I feel the same financially? We spent the extra money we now had on consumer purchases not to saving and investing. That quickly changed. I made an effort to pay my car off within two and one-half years and was able to save and invest more. Now I had savings and a college fund.

Most people do not learn from lifestyle inflation. They look up ten years from now, and they are no better off just deeper in debt. I don't care how many raises or promotions you get, if you are not smart with your money, it will never make a difference in your financial well-being. You will just wind up with a bunch of stuff and no money in the bank.

When you get a raise at work or a windfall, try not to recognize that the money is there (I know that's hard, but stick with me here). Let it sit. Take the increase or at least half of it and put in into savings and pretend that you never received it. If you cannot afford to do that, take 10-15 percent of it and save it. Just get into the habit of saving a part of any money that comes your way.

The ultimate goal as I said earlier is to save 30 percent of your income and force yourself to live off of the remaining 70 percent. YES, this includes taxes and health insurance. If you do this tomorrow, you will go crazy. If you do one percent at a time, you will go crazy. Find a happy medium. Not too slow and not too fast. It's going to hurt at first because you are not used to jacking money from yourself. After a month, you will get acclimated to it. A year later, you will be patting yourself of the back. You will say to yourself, wow this book has changed my life!

If you don't want to change, go back to being broke. However, if you want to have a cushion in the bank, you have to change your saving habits. You are not getting any younger, so start the journey to building wealth NOW.

No one enjoys living paycheck to paycheck. However very few are willing to change. According to the *Wall Street Journal* nearly 70 percent of Americans live paycheck to paycheck. Immediate gratification is the thief of the middle class; -- we want it and we want it now. Why save for something when credit can let you have it faster?

"I want a plasma TV." No problem, just fill out this credit application, and you can have it today. (Don't worry the 20 percent interest.) Anything that is too easy to get, watch out! You will pay a huge price for the convenience and your impatience.

"Buy in haste, repent at leisure"

Some people buy homes and later regret it because they are barely breathing thanks to the extra expenses that a house can bring: home insurance, property taxes, more furniture, higher utility bills, etc.

This gets us into trouble if we spend at the same rate as our income rises we have nothing saved for emergencies. If we live above our pay rate, we will go into debt. We have to then tap the credit card to make ends meet. PRACTICE CONTENTMENT if you can.

I once saw Robert Reich speak on super capitalism; he says America produces more than the average person can keep up with. Our income has not kept up with consumer goods. Therefore, the middle class is steadily shrinking.

For example, in 2007, Apple came out with its iPhone ($499) and created hysteria; about a year later the better, faster 3G iPhone was introduced at $199. If you try to keep up with the latest and greatest, you will always be broke. The average rich person doesn't buy a phone every two years. So what's the solution? Glad you asked. Keep reading.

Try your best to keep your income higher than your expenditures. Watch your spending. Instead of buying an iPhone every few years, buy Apple stock. That's how a capitalist thinks. Think investing instead of consuming all the time. Create a side business. In addition to your job, think of ways to create more income streams. Just don't sit on one income stream forever; I don't care how much you earn. I do not recommend a second job unless you're deep in debt and need a temporary income to pay down the debt. However, do not make it permanent. You will soon get burnt out. A second job should be temporary not a long-term plan.

All in all, the process of changing your relationship with money can be difficult: saving money, paying off debt, and investing to build wealth can just add more stress on top of your day-to-day issues. However, if you want more freedom and comfort in your financial life, you have to take personal responsibility. No one else is going to do it for you.

Fancy cars, fine clothes, and the latest gadgets can always enhance your lifestyle and indeed make you appear rich.

People who are already wealthy can afford to spend a certain amount of their income frivolously, but when you starting out in this wealth building journey take your time. Build assets and then buy your toys.

Most people spend the first ten working years of their life: saving, investing, and creating income streams; the other fifty years they enjoy the fruits of their labor.

The rest spend their first ten years: having fun, getting into debt, and buying things on credit; they spend the remaining fifty years making debt payments.

The first half develop habits to make their future secure, comfortable, and above average.

The rest develop so many spending habits that it becomes hard for them to develop a saving discipline. By the time they realize their bad habits; they're too set in their ways and feel uncomfortable changing their bad habits.

The choice is yours, suffer now or suffer later.

You have a car; you make more money, and what happens: you get a better car. You have a house, you make more money, and you get a bigger house. You have clothes, you make more money, and you get better clothes. With clothes, the exception can be an upper-management job that may require more of an executive style. I can understand that, but in general, as income goes up, we tend to increase our expenses. And you wonder why you are not wealthy.

But hey, you look good and that's all that matters, right?

Be aware, America is filled with advertisements that tell you what to drive, what to wear, and how to live. Try not to be weak and fall for these tactics. Lifestyle Inflation can be damaging so be careful.

Just as soon as people make enough money to live comfortably, they want to live extravagantly

-Anonymous

Guilty Pleasures

We all have them. It may be dining out, nice clothes, shoes, purses, electronics, golfing, or traveling. We can save for these items if need be. The problem with saving is that we run out of patience and spend as if there is no tomorrow. Most of the time we don't have the money, and our eyes are bigger than our paychecks. Plan for these items instead of tapping the credit card, which only shows that you are impatient and not disciplined with your money.

Let's say the new Blackberry phone is hitting stores next month and you (as usual) don't have the $400 to buy it. What are your options?

A. Charge it

B. Save for it ($100 a month for four months)

C. Wait for it to go on sale next year

The best answer is C. Electronic items always go down in value as soon as another model comes out. So why not wait and you will save yourself interest charges from charging it.

You can save for it, but the minute you buy it, it will instantly lose value. If you can wait until the price decreases (and it will decrease), you can probably save $200. So why not wait. The biggest obstacle in getting rich is acting like you're rich. So develop the mentality that you don't have to have the latest gadget the minute it hits the store. Would it kill you, if you upgrade your Blackberry a year later? I doubt it. Start buying items at a discount instead. Ask your current cell carrier for any promotions or discounts for current customers. You don't know until you ask. If not, have patience because the price will indeed go down. We will always have guilty pleasures because we're human. So why not get a good deal on them or do the next best thing—save for them!

Ask for deals

Stop paying full price all the time. This is another way to stay in control of your money. Hotels, car rentals, cell phones, cable, and car insurance are the best places for deals and negotiations. Always ask for deals or lower options.

Electronics, jewelry, and furniture are always overpriced you can certainly negotiate on these items as well.

Get into the habit of being frugal. Please don't take this too far and start asking for stuff free because it then will become tacky.

Always ask "Is this the best price you can give me?"

Becoming an American Automobile Association (AAA) member can also get you discounts on car rental, hotels, and car insurance. When renting a car, there is no need to buy the car rental insurance when you have insurance on your own car. When you go to a department store, always ask for samples of makeup, perfume, or moisturizers.

Correct wording always helps. Do not walk in and ask, "Do you have anything for free?" Have good verbal communication. Always start with "Hi, how are you? I love this _____ (perfume, moisturizer, etc) do you have any samples available?" Do this for your favorite makeup, cologne, moisturizers, etc.

Don't Have Dessert Before Dinner

I'll admit that shopping for new clothes feels good. However, everything should have a balance.

Cookies taste better than vegetables. A banana split tastes better than an Apple. So, of course, we want to taste the sweet stuff first.

But we cannot have dessert before dinner. So take care of *NEEDS* before *WANTS*. Simply put.

We must put things in order if we want to win financially. Take care of utilities and household needs before fun.

It's called being an adult.

When the bills are paid, I don't feel guilty eating lunch out or buying something for myself.

I automate all expenses and investments, except utilities (too volatile) because it's never a fixed amount like our other bills. We pay utilities after we receive the paper bill in the mail, so we can make sure it's accurate.

Only a few bills arrive in our mailbox; I opt out of credit card solicitations because I don't have a credit card and don't have an urge to obtain one anytime soon. Other than the utility bills, there is not much clutter in our mailbox.

Automating (fixed) expenses forces you to take care of important things first. It also enables you to live an uncluttered life.

Have Your Dinner Before Dessert

Pay yourself and your necessary expenses first, and then have your dessert (fun, entertainment).

I cannot say have dinner and skip dessert; life just would not be any fun. Sometimes you need a little dessert.

I don't want you to live in deprivation; this is why most finance books bore people because they do not see the fun in it. Congratulate yourself every now and then. Always allocate a little cash for splurging.

Earn More Than You Spend

Most Americans stretch their lifestyle beyond their income, causing them to go in debt. It is hard to decrease your lifestyle when you have gotten used to living a certain way. If it's too hard for you to cut your lifestyle, try earning more income. (See chapter 3) Think outside (the box) of your job, what other skills do you have? Jump on some social media sites and market yourself! Social media is a great way to market your business. They are the new business cards. Find out what you love to do and create a business from it. Will this happen overnight? Of course not, but at least you're working toward a goal.

CAUTION: Do not leave your job just because you are passionate about something else. Research and figure out a plan to still feed your family while doing what you love. Do not put your family in jeopardy because of failure to plan. Make sure you are not leaving money to go after something that does not take care of your family. The best thing to do is to start part time.

When you earn more than you make, you will always have room to save and invest. If you cannot find a side business to create more income, you may need to look for higher paying job.

It's not your employer responsibility to make you rich, that's your responsibility. Your employer's main goal is to keeps costs down. If your job is not paying you want you want, that is your fault.

> *"You don't get paid what you're worth; you get paid what you ask."*
>
> -Anonymous

Give yourself a raise by making more money outside of your job; it may be faster than waiting on a raise. You can also find a better paying job in your field.

The rich do not depend on a paycheck, so think beyond the paycheck mentality. I never heard of an employer going to an employee and saying, "We discovered we are not paying you enough. Here…take this extra $20,000 a year." Not going to happen. You create your own destiny. Don't wait for someone to do it for you. The more you make, the more you can SAVE.

Most books use the cliché spend less than you earn. I decided to flip it around; I say, "Earn more than you spend," so that you can focus on the *earning* part. When you force yourself to spend less than you earn, you will never see any alternatives to the solution. All you learn is how to cut expenses. There is a limit to cutting expenses; you can only go down so far. However, there's no limit to the income you can make. I want your income to go up as your debt load decreases making that surplus yours to keep. I was also doing this during my hiatus from incurring debt and visiting the mall.

Keep income up and keep debt low. As you do this, you will have more money to keep.

```
Income
|          )
|          )  ----→ all this is yours
|          )
|          )
|
|debt
|_____
```

Got it? Good!

Personally I think it's easier to earn more than to cut expenses. When you cut expenses you start to feel squeezed and uncomfortable. When you earn more, you are moving forward, and you then have more wiggle room to fight debt and other expenses.

When you concentrate on living below your means, you are focusing on cutting expenses to the bare minimum, which leaves you less focused on upgrading your income.

When I was making a meager salary fresh out of college, I was earning more than I spent. A few years later, I decided to buy a brand new car because I thought a college graduate should not be riding around in a used car. From that point on, I began getting poorer and poorer because my expenses were higher than my income. In college, I had a simple lifestyle. When I graduated, I doubled my income, which made me double my expenses. The trick is to keep your income up and your debt low. Today I am earning way more than I spend, now I can save much more and have a better standard of living, including traveling abroad, a nicer car, a home, and other toys.

So replace living below your means with earning more than you spend. Psychologically, you will put yourself in a position to keep making more money.

A person who makes $150,000 a year can have a better standard of living, than a person making $30,000, even though both are living below their means.

So in addition to getting the average advice of living below your means, earn more as well. Don't just do one without doing the other, DO BOTH! Now you're above average.

I knew a guy who once saved and invested his entire net income from his full time job. He was able to do that because he was living in a multifamily unit, and his renters were paying his mortgage. He was also doing consulting work on the side to maintain his day-to-day expenses. Try to work on both ends if you want to get ahead financially. Save and earn more! He was able to save his full income by keeping expenses low and at the same time he found a way to earn more money through his other talents.

Part-time employment can be a short term fix. A bonus or raise can also soothe the burden. However, a better-paying job can really put things in to overdrive.

Depending on how focused you are and how fast you want to get out of debt, you could try both earning while cutting your expenses. If you want to really get a head start, sell stuff you no longer need or use, adjust your withholdings on your W-4 form at work, and decrease your 401k deductions temporarily. Those are all fast moves to make.

Disgusted that you have to do all these things? This should make you never want to have consumer debt again. You cannot grow rich by borrowing more to pay for things. Take action and pay your debt off.

Stay focused, and do not get discouraged!

If you want to get drastic, move! Again, housing and car payments are usually the largest monthly debt a person has. You can get very drastic and downsize in these two areas.

Take my model for instance; this is how to get ahead and not just get by:

It's all about percentages, once they are out of whack, you don't have a chance of getting ahead regardless of how big your income may be.

Your take home monthly income should be within these percentages:

Less than 30 percent mortgage/rent

10 percent transportation (gas, car note, oil change, car registration, and insurance)

10 percent household needs

For example, if you make $50,000 a year, $500/month should be geared to transportation costs, and, yes, this includes your car note.

If you cannot remember the percentages for each category, just try to remember all your basic needs should be 50 percent or lower.

The rest can go toward savings/investments and other daily expenses and of course taxes. As I said before, I personally save/invest/give 30 percent of my income. You can start with less and work your way up.

So if you make a fat income ($100,000 or more) and are broke every month, it's not your income. There's a big chance that your percentages are not in order. What makes a person squeeze his entire income into the basic needs categories and not a penny going to savings/investments? It's usually your consumer debt that is taking up our savings/investments percentages.

Most people are still able to pay their bills regardless of this perfect model, but they are just getting by and not getting ahead.

Adjust your percentages if you want to get ahead!

Your spending

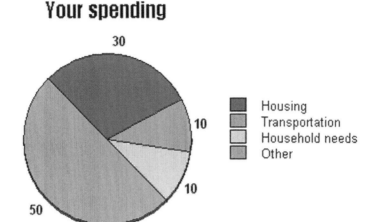

Other expenses may include obligations such as insurance, food, and discretionary spending such as taxi rides, lattes, dry cleaning, and entertainment.

Of course, it's easier to keep your mortgage under 30 percent when you don't have consumer debt. It's a perfect model, but it does not hurt to strive for it.

Don't like the picture. Earn more income. In Larry Winget's book, *You're Broke Because You Want to Be*, he says people spend money on things based on what is important to them. If it's important for you to look cool, you may be driving a car with a heavy car note. If looking cute is important to you, your money may be going to big retailers to spend on clothes. Take personal responsibility for your life.

What's important to me?

My Retirement
My Business
Money in the Bank
My Child's Education

Culture and Arts
Traveling

This is where the excess of my money goes once my family needs are taken care of. Decide what is important to you. There can be more room to splurge, once your debt is eliminated or under control.

Chapter 5: Take It up a Notch

Once you have the gist of saving, debt control, and investing under your belt, you are in the position to start taking risks. It's time for you to take it to the next level.

Always, always have more than one stream of income. Don't just sit on your job. Create more streams. I don't care how well your job pays you; get into the habit of making more than your job gives you.

To become wealthy, you have to take more risks—invest, real estate, or build a business. You may have to flirt a little with business debt. As long as you have a plan, do your research, and can make a decent return on your investment, take the plunge! If it's too risky, continue saving money.

Comfortable ----> job, income, little savings, and 401k

Secure ----> large cash savings

Rich ----> a business

You need all three to be well-balanced.

If you like to day trade, make sure you have secure cash savings before you risk your money. In other words, make sure you trade with money you can "afford" to lose.

If you're going to start a business, do not use your life savings to start it. Start slowly.

If you want to buy individual stocks, make sure you have a long-term strategy (401k, IRA) in plan first.

Have a backup plan when you take risk, do not take all-or-nothing type risks, and make sure each risk is well calculated.

I will also like to add that risk taking (the rich stage) comes after you are secure and comfortable. If you are single with no kids, you probably can afford to be more aggressive.

These are all factors of building wealth:

Income (job)

Saving money (a set percentage from your paycheck going to a savings account.

Investing (a set percentage from your paycheck going to a 401k, index mutual funds, stocks, or real estate).

Entrepreneurship (starting/building a business)

Save a portion of your income. Mix it with investing in the stock market and starting a side business that will eventually grow your assets.

Job + Savings + Investing + a business = Moola!

Apply it and keep repeating; you will start to be in control of your life, instead of life controlling you. As John Commuta says in his audio book *Transforming Debt into Wealth* you need to define your success or it will be defined for you by the people that want your money.

Keep striving and remain patient; it usually takes the average person fifteen to twenty years to become wealthy!

Your permanent goal is to develop a wealthy mindset

The rich save over 15 percent of their income
the poor do not.

The rich avoid consumer debt;
the poor embrace it, which makes them fall behind financially.

The poor buy on emotion, while
the rich practice discipline.

The poor have a case of lifestyle debt, but
the rich have business debt.

The poor spend money on their external minds—flamboyant.

The rich spend money on their inner self (reading and investing in self-development.)

The rich are concerned about creating wealth for generations.

The poor and middle class are concerned about looking cool (having the latest car or latest technology). Again, they're flamboyant.

Save and buy assets first then spend it on liabilities and/or expenses.

Three stages of your financial life:

Poor - a job, i.e., survival, to feed, and clothe yourself

Middle class - a career, i.e., comfort and advancement

Rich - a business; build real estate and stock portfolios

Think about what category that attracts you. Let me explain each of them.

It does not require much skills or education to get a job. A job is something many people can get. A quick interview and drug screen are the usual requirements. These are typically easy to get but hard to stay in because of the low pay, morale, and/or poor promotions.

A career requires more education, more analytical thinking, and more skills. Most careers require a college degree and some require graduate degrees. Careers are more fulfilling to mature Americans because they typically pay well and have good benefits, such as health, life, dental, and vision insurance. Your choices for promotions are clear, and the morale is usually high. Married individuals with families seek careers because the pay can be above average and can give you a quality standard of living.

A business can reinvent your success. Business owners are people that don't like being told what to do. There are not mentally fit to work for someone else (and I mean this in a good way). They are leaders and risk takers, innovators. They love turning nothing into something. They love what they do and are willing to sacrifice long hours and time away from their family to grow their empire. Unlike the career person, business owners work because they love to, not necessary for the money. It normally takes a longer time to make money in a business compared to a career, but the results are so much better. Instead retiring at an old age, business owners can retire earlier than someone with a career or job but choose not to. They are loyal to their workers instead of a job. They work to serve others instead of a boss. The rewards are plentiful. Hours can be flexible once the business is in a mature stage, and each day can bring more excitement than a day-to-day career path. The best part anyone can start a business, no college degree required.

Each stage has its ups and downs; it all depends on what type of person you are. However, you are sure to become rich with a successful business than a successful career. Your standard of living is also richer in quality.

A business requires a lot of work and research up front, and it can take years before any real money is pocketed. A career and job requires social capital up front: a polished resume and great interview skills. So the choice is yours; you can be a plumber or have a plumbing business. Be a teacher or open up a school. Be a computer programmer or an IT consultant.

Chapter 6: Your Spouse and Money

Honey, let's live on one salary!

This is another way to accelerate your savings. Use the larger paycheck to pay the bills, day-to-day expenses, and household needs, and save the other spouse's paycheck.

I know, I know that maybe impossible or you are probably saying, "I wish you had told me this when we were first married. My husband is nuts already, he will not go for this."

During the recession, a lot of couples weathered the storm simply by using this strategy. When you are doing smart things, as times are good, you can reap the benefits when times are bad. With one spouse laid off, the stress is not apparent if you were living on one salary to begin with.

In order to make this strategy work, you may want to downsize or decrease your lifestyle a little. Remember I'm not saying do all this by tomorrow. But at least start the journey. There are few people that are doing this and are not regretting it. Just imagine having all the extra savings, now you can easily start a college fund, have money for emergencies, have a retirement fund, or money for vacations all at once. It all comes down to discipline. You cannot get something for nothing.

Playing the lottery and entering sweepstakes are never wise choice; it's your job to control of your own destiny.

Also living on one income can teach you contentment. Not buying everything you see is practicing contentment and in just a few months, you can pile up cash faster. Being in America, I know it's hard, commercials and billboards encourage us every day to spend money. Everybody wants our money; few companies encourage us to save. In addition to spending, we live for today and deal with tomorrow when it comes.

You are not getting any younger, so take control of your financial life.

Financial Abandonment

Yes, I have to talk about this. If you don't want to read this you can skip this section.

Do not abandon your spouse financially. Yes, one can make sure the bills are paid on time, but too often I hear where one spouse takes the entire financial burden of the household, while the other does not know what's going on. When you dump the financial responsibilities on your partner, he or she goes through the most stress. If you don't know or have a clue what bills the household has you are indeed financially abandoning your partner. "But my husband/wife is not financially literate. He/she is better taking care of the kids or better at fixing up the house than managing it." Your partner does not need to start paying bills but should know what's going on. If you have $2,000 in medical bills, she/he needs to at least have knowledge that the bill does exist. If you both want to visit Bermuda, you both need to know how much will it costs and what is needed for the hotel and airfare. Keep your partner informed of every financial bill and/or decision that will affect the household.

If you are the one who's carrying the weight, you need to communicate more with your spouse. I often hear, "Well my wife handles the bills, and I just make the money." You need to know if your income matches the expenses of the household. Don't be oblivious to the situation. "Well, she never mentioned that anything was wrong, so I figured we were okay." Don't guess; find out for sure. She may be scared to tell you that you both have $20,000 in debt because this may start an argument. You have to speak openly on this subject. When you are married, it's hard for both of you to get ahead when one is not supportive. This will start to affect other areas of your life as well.

I know people who just go to work everyday and don't care where the money goes because they have no financial plans or goals. They feel that they are doing well. Meanwhile, they can have $50,000 in credit card debt. They're spending everyday without looking at the bank account balance, and when they run out of cash, they turn to the credit card to fill in the gaps.

This is a lousy way to live. Communicate on money at least twice a month.

Also don't neglect your family just to reach a goal. Yes, stay focused; just don't deprive your loved ones just to reach a goal. Pace yourself and work on the plan with your spouse. Both of you should be in agreement about your goal. You don't want to get in the cycle of get married, go deep in debt, and get divorced."

I understand that when you are already in the hole, it's hard to dig yourself out; to save, invest, and build wealth seems out of the question. We tend to throw in the towel because money problems pile up, and we give up prematurely. Anything worth having takes time. Financial security does not come easy—unless you come from rich parents.

We all have different starting points when it comes to debt; here are a few:

We're too much in debt; we don't have a chance at getting ahead.

For those of you that are in five-figure debt excluding the house, you are not an exception—you are as normal as the rest of

American society. The average person walking around has debt. You are in the majority. Now the question is: what are you going to do about it? Are you going to wallow in debt or find a way out? Yes, it's going to take time, and it's hard. But good things do not come easy. Start by making a list of all your debts. Which ones can you pay this month without sacrificing basic household needs? Each time you get a paycheck, list the debts that are due and pay them accordingly. If you are still short, adjust your withholdings on your W-2 form. Still short?—a second job is needed.

I have $18,000 in debt and no savings.

Yes, it is possible that you may not see the light because you are overwhelmed. You should probably just focus on the next two weeks and getting to the next pay period.

Focus on the debt and break it down; while you are pecking away debt add some to savings. You can save as little as 5 percent of your income. There is no one-size-fits-all plan. If you like accomplishing fast results, pay the smallest debt first. If you rather pay the highest interest rate off, by all means do it. Sell stuff on eBay or Craigslist. I advise you to pay more than the minimum; the longer you stay in debt, the longer it takes you to move on to other savings and investment vehicles.

I have an outstanding lien, and now I'm having my paycheck garnished.

Liens are more serious than ordinary past due accounts. I suggest that you call the law firm on the lawsuit papers and negotiate a payment plan. Possibly they will stop the garnishment, just remember to get everything in writing.

I owe the IRS thousands!

If you have a credit card with enough available credit to pay off the IRS, please use it. I'd rather have the amount owed to a credit card company than to the IRS. Yes, you just transferred the debt and nothing has changed. But the IRS has tremendous power and can put a lien on your checking account without notice or garnished your wages without suing you. Trust me; you don't want the IRS on your back. If you don't have a credit card, simply call the IRS and work out a payment plan; don't let interest and penalties pile up. Please seek and do these steps yourself; there's no need to find a tax attorney and pay them to do the things you can do yourself

Can I just roll my debt into a home equity line?

Yes you can, but what sense does that make? You have not done anything but simply move the debt to another creditor. Why don't you just get out of debt the same way you got into it—knock it out a little at a time. You miss a payment on your credit card, and you will get hounded with phone calls. If you miss a payment on your home equity line, your house will be in jeopardy of foreclosure. Leave the equity in your house alone.

My spouse tends to overspend when it comes to the kids.

I often hear of four-year-olds and even younger children having stellar birthday parties costing, upwards of $600. The pony, clown, food, and more entertainment all add up. When you are in debt, you have to balance your fun. Some people were raised, not having these things so they make up for it through their children. When you are raised without much discretionary income, you may wind up going to the extreme when it comes to spending, or you may go the opposite way and become super frugal because this is the only world you know. Having a spouse like this can cause additional arguments. The ones that are loose spenders have the attitude of nothing is too good for my child. Remember everything must have a balance; if you are willing to spend hundreds of dollars or more on a birthday party, you should be prepared to cut expenses elsewhere. It's important that both spouses are in agreement with big-ticket items. If not, try to come to a happy medium. When you do not set boundaries with children, they grow up not respecting money. Giving children everything they want is not always good.

We're behind on every single bill. We are not current on anything!

The first bill you want to remain current on is your rent/mortgage. Food is also important. Next are utilities, then transportation. These are your four walls. Pay these bills first. If there is money leftover concentrate on the other debts, list all your bills from the lowest amount you owe to the highest balance you have. Concentrate on the lowest bill and use your funds toward that bill…NOW. Don't delay; start this process with your next paycheck. Once the debt is paid, go to the next bill and repeat. Do not spend a dime on any leisure activities or entertainment. Just concentrate on the bill. When you focus solely on your debt and monthly expenses, you will eventually get ahead. If you do not make enough money to take care of your four walls, you may need to move to a less expensive neighborhood or downgrade your transportation. It's may be quicker to do this than to make more income. Most of the time the problem is not our income is usually our expenses.

I am six figures in debt and on the verge of divorce.

If this is something you created behind your spouse's back, he or she has every right to be angry. If you both took this ride together, your spouse needs to stick it out with you if he or she truly loves you. Money problems can always mess up a marriage. Try to continue to love your partner. Find a way out; you may need to expand your income streams for extra income. If you cannot do that, you may want to work out a payment plan. However, regardless of your debt, your basic living expenses should be paid first before you pay any creditor. Basic living includes: Housing, Food, Utilities and Transportation.

From there, if there is any cash remaining, it may go to debt. This is not the time to worry about your credit score.

If you are unable to pay your creditors, they will have to wait. You deal with them when you're able to increase your income. When your income goes up, then you can work out a payment plan; by that time, the creditors maybe willing to take a lump-sum payment and dismiss the remaining portion of the bill. In some cases fifty cents on the dollar. Work on the things you can control. Don't work on what you can't control.

Credit counseling can also help:

Visit Consumer Credit Counseling Service http://www.cccs-inc.org or call 1-866-889-9347 or *National Foundation for Credit Counseling (NFCC) 1-800-388-2227* to speak to a counselor

Whatever your case may be, do not try to let it overburden you to the point that you cannot sleep or eat because having health problems would make it worse.

Remember these are things, and family and friends are more important assets than material things.

Bottom line: Focus and don't worry what others think. Change your mentality, and the rest will follow.

It's best to tackle debt in the beginning stages before it swells and multiplies. Usually when a person gets a credit card and uses it, if it's not paid off within the first bill cycle, it may never be paid off. This is when the debt cycle begins.

Change your thinking. Think in terms of building wealth instead of paying minimum payments!

It took you awhile to get into this debt, so it may take awhile to get out or at least get it manageable.

Kids and Money

Setting a good example for children takes all the fun out of middle age.

-William Feather

Most kids are never taught how to handle money. They need to have firsthand experience to learn smart money management skills, and without the money, there is no experience.

This is how an allowance fits in. Financial adviser David McCurrach, Founder of Kids' Money, surveyed parents and found that about 60 percent give their kids an allowance.

You can show your kids how to use their allowance by dividing it into these three categories:

Giving - Church or charitable donations or birthday presents.

Spending – Candy, games, specialty clothing items, and entertainment.

Saving - A percent of their allowance needs to be put toward any items they wish to obtain but cannot afford at the moment.

It's one thing to give your children money and another to actually teach them about money and how to manage it.

Once they start asking for stuff, it's time! It's worth the time and effort to teach them and it may save you years of supporting adult children in the future. Giving an allowance without chores attached to it is a waste. Teach them nothing comes for free and work produces income. Don't just give them an allowance without chores.

Chapter 7: Grow and explore

Career

The average household income in the United States is $50,233 according to the U.S. Census Bureau.

It is up to you; you can be average or above average. It also been said that $50,000 is the point where we tend to be the most happy.

When earning beyond $50,000 a year, I guess we just want more toys or a higher luxury of living. People who move from $40,000 to 50,000 a year increase their level of happiness, but an increase from $50,000 to $60,000 made no impact. Once you have all your needs, it becomes more of a wanting game after that or just keeping score. I'm not telling you to keep your score at $50,000. But don't expect a wave of happiness after an income of $50,000. You will just have more options.

So think about it for a while—$50,000 is the magic number for contentment. So choosing an income over $50,000 a year may not bring any more happiness; in fact you may begin to create more debt as your income rises. So choose a career that makes you happy first and the money will soon follow. Or take the money first and do what makes you passionate/happy on the side.

Good sites for job searching:

www.careeerbuilder.com
www.indeed.com
www.dice.com (information technology jobs)

No matter how many degrees or technical skills you have, the number-one asset one can have when looking for a job is not a degree, certifications, or leadership skills. The number-one asset that can help you land a great job is social skills—a must have for anyone. So work hard on this skill. I notice it comes easy for some and yet hard for introverts, but it can be the breaking point on most interviews. So practice, practice, practice. If there are two candidates interviewing for the same position, considering both have the same experience and education, if the interviewer is not socially comfortable with you the other candidate may get the job. Also learn how to adapt to change. This asset also is a plus. We live in an age where technology and the environment changes all the time. Learn or you will get left behind.

Are you ready for an interview?

Here are some steps you can take when preparing for an interview:

Arrive early—fifteen minutes early to be exact.

Bring a nice briefcase or shoulder bag with two pens (in case one runs out of ink) and a notepad. Keep a folder with your resume, and references in it.

Check yourself before you leave the house; make sure your clothes are neat and presentable. And check again in the mirror before you start the interview. Check your breath. Have a mint fifteen minutes before the interview.

Speak clearly during the interview; have a drink of water and clear your throat before you meet with the interviewer.

Do a trial run the day before the interview. Time yourself on how long it takes to get to the location of the interview. You don't want to be late and asking for directions, on the day of the interview.

Know how to properly pronounce the interviewer's first and last name. Keep repeating it, so you will get it right. Also at the end of the interview remember his/her name and thank the interviewer.

Please leave your cell phone in the car! No interruptions.

Negotiate salary

This is best when you are first offered the position—yes, get your money up front. It has been said that men are better at negotiating salaries than women.

Men are known to always ask for more money when offered a job. Women want to be nice. Women! This is a new era. When it comes to money, you should become more aggressive. Most hiring managers have a 15 percent cushion to go higher when giving job offers. So go for it. Make sure you have a good reason to ask for more money. Seek out different resources on educating yourself on pay raises.

> *Education: The shortest distance between wealth and poverty*
>
> *-Robert G. Allen*

Chapter 8: Protect your wealth

Life Insurance

Having life insurance protects your nest egg. If you die, your spouse and family should have enough money and not have to dip into your investments, home equity, or to go into debt. Life insurance is one of the most essential ways you can protect your nest egg. If you have anyone depending on your income, you need Life insurance. I recommend *term life* insurance because it is very simple and inexpensive. A twenty-year term period is enough. Twenty years is enough time for you to build wealth and raise your kids to live independently. After twenty years, you should have built up wealth and assets to pay off any outstanding liabilities.

If you are single with no dependants having insurance through your employer may be *sufficient* enough. Also be honest when giving your medical history! Most life insurance policies have an *incontestability clause,* which means policies have the right to contest payment if you were to die within the first two years of creating the policy. For example, if you were to die from lung cancer, which resulted from you smoking, and you were not honest and upfront about your habit, when you established the policy, they have the right to not pay your beneficiaries. You must be completely honest when answering medical questions.

You may also want to review your policy. Some polices do not cover dangerous sports/hobbies such as aviation, mountain climbing, diving, motor sports, and parachuting.

Most people want enough insurance to pay off the house and any outstanding bills.

How much insurance do you need? Five to ten times your income is sufficient, i.e.; a person with a $50,000 income would need no more than $500,000 of insurance.

Disability Insurance

Yeah, you may need this, too. This is also vital. Again if there is someone who depends on you financially, you need to have this in place. Disability insurance can also protect your wealth. By having disability insurance, it less you need to depend on other sources. Insurance usually pays about 60 percent of your income. Why 60 percent and not a 100 percent? Good question because you do not take home 100 percent of your income. Once taxes and medical insurance are taken out you only take home about 60 percent. Disability insurance is based on net income not gross. Also you should be already adjusting your lifestyle to live on 50 percent of your income, right? (See chapter 2.)

Short-term disability starts after a claim is made but ends within two years. Long-term takes longer to start, from thirty-one days to a time set by you but can last until your death. Disability insurance coupled with a healthy emergency fund can also protect you from cashing out your retirement and/or investment accounts.

Wills

Yes, we all are going to die someday. Of course everyone needs a will as soon as one starts to build assets, even if you have no children. Yes, by law your assets go to your spouse or next to kin. But if someone contests it, guess what? Your spouse may be waiting for a long time to get your assets. If you want him or her to have a smooth transition to inheriting your assets without it going through a lengthy probate process, get a will!

I also suggest if your partner is not financially astute, try educating him or her on how to access information regarding the family policies. You may want to have instructions, passwords, and bank account numbers listed on a sheet on paper stored somewhere safe, so they can have directions on where to find other information.

How to write a will? You can go to any office supply store and get a preprinted form, fill it out, and have it notarized; you can also go to a lawyer and have a will drafted. This may take a couple of weeks. Lawyers typically charge a flat fee of $300-$1000 for this service.

Giving

Giving is a significant part of staying wealthy. It's a personal decision but an important one. When you give, it tends to come back you. Almost like karma. Giving is very important to me. Regardless if you make $20,000 or $200,000 a year, you should always give a portion of your income. You can give to your religion or give to charitable organizations. How much is up to you. When I was broke, I still managed to give a portion of my income. Sometimes it was as little as $10. Get into the habit of giving no matter how small.

One of my favorite charities is DonorsChoose.org. If you are unsure where to give, you can start with the Better Business Bureau Web site www.bbb.org/us/charity. The Web site provides a list of all charitable causes.

The best way to enjoy spending is to GIVE; I have received the best feeling just by giving money to my favorite causes:

Donor's Choose	www.donorschoose.org
Charity: Water	www.charitywater.org
Boys and Girls Club of America	www.bgca.org

I'm a big education buff. As Oprah once said, when you donate to education, you aren't just helping one person; you are helping a family because a person with an education can help his or her entire family.

Give Back

Remember: People first. Karma can work both ways: good or bad.

Giving a part of your earnings is essential to wealth building and is also good karma.

In Summary

All the advice I suggest will not happen overnight, however, the wisdom of being smart with your money helps you smooth out the process of being financially savvy.

We all have been taught to pay ourselves first. Get a bunch of insurance, save for this and save for that, and not pile up debt, plus enjoy life and have fun. Most people cannot do it all perfectly. Be diligent and have patience, and you can receive the best that life has to offer.

When you visit a furniture store, I promise you the best the store has to offer will always be centered in front of the store; this is the case with most retail stores. Next season there will be a different setup. My point is, if you keep up with fashion and the latest trend, you will never become wealthy. It will never be enough. Practice contentment, and you will see your money grow. Make it a habit to proactively save and invest on a monthly basis systematically. In other words, look out for yourself before the profit of any retailer.

> *The bottom line is that we think we work to pay the bills, we spend more than we need on things we really don't need? This sends us back to work to get more stuff.*
>
> -Joe Dominguez, *Your Money or Your Life*

I have an idea, work to buy what you need and save a percentage for emergencies. Always put spending last. Investing should always be first, if you want to be wealthy. If you want to be average, follow the crowd. Save and invest before you spend. This is a good habit to have.

Having money gives you more options and more opportunities for building your goals or dreams. You may want to save for a house, rental property or perhaps to start a business. Having good saving habits sets the stage to become rich. So first you must lay down a good foundation (stable income), save, and invest until you're at a comfortable position to leap out on your own. Or you can do both, work on covering your needs and work part time on your empire. Each day is a new opportunity to work on your dreams/goals. I know it's hard when you have a family opposed to a single person, but you have to make the effort and sacrifice if you choose to be rich. It's not easy, but it's worth it. What's easy is being average. Picking a great spouse can be the most important thing you can do. So you want to get it right the first time. When you have an understanding spouse, you have a survivor on your team. This can be a choice that can make or break you. So pick wisely.

In becoming wealthy, dismiss what the media portrays: ridiculous spending, private jets, flashy cars, fine dining, and massive jewelry. Actually, I'll take the fine dining part, but the rest is misleading. I'm not teaching you to be flamboyant; I'm teaching you how to make your money grow and to preserve it. It comes down to what makes you feel comfortable. Personal finance is, well, *personal*. Make the best decision for you and your family. There are several ways to become wealthy. Choosing to be wealthy is the first step.

> *Rich people plan for three generations*
> *Poor people plan for Saturday night*
>
> -Gloria Steinman

Have fun choosing,

L. Marie Joseph

BONUS

Have a greater purpose in life.

Once you have set the stage for having a great financial future, you have to set some personal goals that are nonfinancial. It makes no sense to be rich or on your way to becoming rich without having a greater purpose in life. Take time out to set goals that are more in line with your values. Maybe it's volunteering at a school or running a marathon. Even millionaires have hobbies aside from making money. I once volunteered with low-income communities and gave away computers. I also volunteered at my local library. Find out what you are passionate about. It maybe writing poetry or writing a novel. You have to balance your life in other areas in addition to having financial fulfillment. You also have to feed your mind spirituality and mentally.

Appendix

Tips on getting ahead

Housing

Twenty-five percent of your income should be going to housing, if you want to get ahead financially. You can increase as far as 30 percent. Over 30 percent is a risk zone

Your home should be no more than two and one-half times your annual salary. Two times if you want to be wealthy.

Savings

You should be saving thirty percent of your income. You can start saving in the following categories: long-term savings, short-term saving, and giving.

Investments

Index funds are excellent.

Look for mutual funds that have five years or more history and a stable management track record with low fees.

ETFs are good as well, but they are mainly for lump-sum investing not for dollar cost average (DCA) investing. Because they are like stocks, there is a charge when buying and selling ETFs, and you pay your broker the same commission that you'd pay on any regular trade. So if you plan to invest a set amount of dollars a month remember that each month you're paying a transaction fee.

Where to Invest

Vanguards, Fidelity, T. Rowe Price are all good brokerage firms for mutual funds and ETFs.

Research Tools for Investing

TD Ameritrade

www.tdameritrade.com

Click on Research & Ideas then Mutual Funds

Insurance: Protect Your Nest Egg

Life – Term life insurance, five to ten times your income, and a twenty-year term.

Disability- pays at least 60 percent of your current income. It takes about three weeks to kick in.

Health- If your employer does not offer it; find the highest deductible, so you can have lower payments.

Sources:

www.insweb.com

www.insurance.com

www.ehealthinsurance.com

Having the proper insurance in place saves you from dipping into your retirement funds and other savings.

Current interest rate for Mortgage and Car loans

www.bankrate.com

Credit Report and Monitoring

You are allowed one free credit report per year.

www.annualcreditreport.com

Debt Counseling

www.nfcc.org

800-388-2227

Estate Planning

Wills

Go to an office supply store and get a preprinted will and testament form. Fill out and get it notarized. Or visit a local attorney to draw up the papers. Be prepared to spend a flat fee of $300-$1,000.

Career-Salary Comparison Tools

Payscale   www.payscale.com
Salary   www.salary.com

Tax Shelters:

<u>Retirement</u>

401k
Solo 401k – for freelancers or contractors
403b - for public education organizations, some nonprofit employers
457 plans - retirement for government employee

Traditional IRA

Roth IRA

SEP - ideal for self employed individuals who own their own company

SPOUSAL IRA - an IRA that is set up for a work-at-home parent with contribution made by the working spouse

<u>College Funds</u>

Kid's college saving plans - 529 or ESA

<u>Charities</u>

Charitable giving - as long as you contribute to a qualified *tax-exempt* organization, which is a 501c organization, this can be tax deductible.

Money Management

Mint www.mint.com

Additional Resources

www.firstgenerationwhitecollar.com

Author Biography

L. Marie Joseph (www.lmariejoseph.com) is a first generation college graduate that entered the workforce without having a clue what to do with her new found income. Through successful strategies and investing she has manage to break the chain of consuming and started building wealth for her family. Marie is a personal finance blogger whose work has been mentioned in *MSN Money, WalletPop, and Forbes Woman.* She is the founder of moneymonk.net, a personal finance blog. She lives in Atlanta with her husband and young daughter.